Mike McGrath

JAVA

fifth edition
covers Java 8

In easy steps is an imprint of In Easy Steps Limited
16 Hamilton Terrace · Holly Walk · Leamington Spa
Warwickshire · United Kingdom · CV32 4LY
www.ineasysteps.com

Fifth Edition

In Easy Steps Limited supports The Forest Stewardship Council (FSC),
the leading international forest certification organisation. All our titles
that are printed on Greenpeace approved FSC certified paper carry the
FSC logo.

MIX
Paper from
responsible sources
FSC
www.fsc.org   FSC® C020837

Printed and bound in the United Kingdom

ISBN 978-1-84078-621-7

Contents

Preface

The creation of this book has provided me, Mike McGrath, a welcome opportunity to update my previous books on Java programming with the latest techniques. All examples I have given in this book demonstrate Java features supported by current compilers on both Windows and Linux operating systems, and the book's screenshots illustrate the actual results produced by compiling and executing the listed code.

Conventions in this book

In order to clarify the code listed in the steps given in each example, I have adopted certain colorization conventions. Components of the Java language itself are colored blue, programmer-specified names are red, numeric and string values are black, and comments are green, like this:

```
// Store then output a text string value.
String message = "Welcome to Java programming!" ;
System.out.println( message ) ;
```

Additionally, in order to identify each source code file described in the steps, a colored icon and file name appears in the margin alongside the steps, like these:

App.java   App.class   App.jar   App.jnlp

Grabbing the source code

For convenience, I have placed source code files from the examples featured in this book into a single ZIP archive. You can obtain the complete archive by following these easy steps:

1. Browse to **http://www.ineasysteps.com** then navigate to the "Free Resources" menu and choose the "Downloads" item

2. Find "Java in easy steps, 5th Edition" in the list, then click on the hyperlink entitled "All Code Examples" to download the archive

3. Now, extract the archive contents to any convenient location on your computer

I sincerely hope you enjoy discovering the programming possibilities of Java and have as much fun with it as I did in writing this book.

Mike McGrath

1 Getting started

Welcome to the exciting world of Java programming. This chapter shows how to create and execute simple Java programs and demonstrates how to store data within programs.

Introduction

The Java™ programming language was first developed in 1990 by an engineer at Sun Microsystems named James Gosling. He was unhappy using the C++ programming language so he created a new language that he named "Oak", after the oak tree that he could see from his office window.

As the popularity of the World Wide Web grew, Sun recognized that Gosling's language could be developed for the internet. Consequently, Sun renamed the language "Java" (simply because that name sounded cool) and made it freely available in 1995. Developers around the world quickly adopted this exciting new language and, because of its modular design, were able to create new features that could be added to the core language. The most endearing additional features were retained in subsequent releases of Java as it developed into the comprehensive version of today.

The essence of Java is a library of files called "classes", which each contain small pieces of ready-made proven code. Any of these classes can be incorporated into a new program, like bricks in a wall, so that only a relatively small amount of new code ever needs to be written to complete the program. This saves the programmer a vast amount of time and largely explains the huge popularity of Java programming. Additionally, this modular arrangement makes it easier to identify any errors than in a single large program.

Java technology is both a programming language and a platform. In Java programming the source code is first written as human-readable plain text files ending with the **.java** extension. These are compiled into machine-readable **.class** files by the **javac** compiler. The **java** interpreter can then execute the program with an instance of the Java Virtual Machine (Java VM):

The New icon pictured above indicates a new or enhanced feature introduced with the latest version of Java.

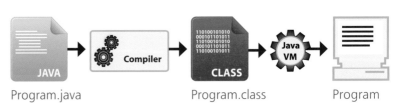

Program.java   Program.class   Program

As the Java VM is available on many different operating systems the same **.class** files are capable of running on Windows, Linux and Mac operating systems – so Java programmers theoretically enjoy the cross-platform ability to "write once, run anywhere".

...cont'd

In order to create Java programs, the Java class libraries and the **javac** compiler need to be installed on your computer. In order to run Java programs, the Java™ Runtime Environment (JRE) needs to be installed to supply the **java** interpreter. All of these components are contained in a freely available package called the Java™ Platform, Standard Edition <u>D</u>evelopment <u>K</u>it (JDK).

The Java programs in this book use version JDK 8, which incorporates both the Development Kit itself and the Runtime Environment, that can be downloaded from the Oracle® website at **http://www.oracle.com/technetwork/java/javase/downloads**

The Oracle download page also features other packages, but only the JDK 8 package is required to get started with Java programming.

The JDK 8 package is available in versions for 32-bit and 64-bit variants of the Linux, Mac, Solaris and Windows platforms – accept the Oracle License Agreement, then select the appropriate version for your computer to download the Java Development Kit.

There is no truth in the rumor that JAVA stands for "Just Another Vague Acronym".

Java SE Development Kit 8		
Thank you for accepting the Oracle Binary Code License Agreement for Java SE; you may now download this software.		
Product / File Description	File Size	Download
Linux x86	152.47 MB	⬇ jdk-8-linux-i586.tar.gz
Linux x64	133.85 MB	⬇ jdk-8-linux-x64.rpm
Mac OS X x64	207.72 MB	⬇ jdk-8-macosx-x64.dmg
Solaris x64	93.15 MB	⬇ jdk-8-solaris-x64.tar.gz
Windows x86	151.68 MB	⬇ jdk-8-windows-i586.exe
Windows x64	155.14 MB	⬇ jdk-8-windows-x64.exe

Installing the JDK

Select the appropriate Java Development Kit package for your system from the Oracle® downloads page and then follow these steps to install Java on your computer:

1 Uninstall any previous versions of the JDK and/or Java Runtime Environment from your system

2 Start the installation and accept the License Agreement

Beware

A previous version of the JRE may be installed so your web browser can run Java applets. It is best to uninstall this to avoid confusion with the newer version in JDK8.

3 When the Custom Setup dialog appears either accept the suggested installation location or click the Change button to choose your preferred location, such as **C:\Java** for Windows systems or **/usr/Java** for Linux systems

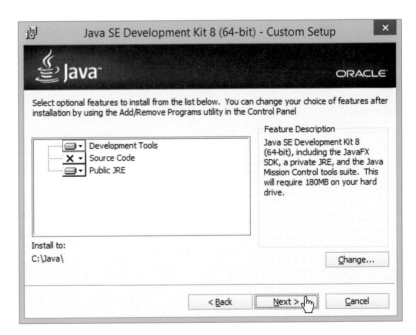

Hot tip

You can start out by installing just the minimum features to avoid confusion.

4 Ensure that the Development Tools and Public JRE features are selected from the list. Optionally, you may deselect the other features as they are not required to start programming with this book

5 Click the Next button to install all the necessary Java class libraries and tools at the chosen location

The tools to compile and run Java programs are normally operated from a Command Prompt and are located in the **bin** sub-directory of the Java directory. These can be made available from anywhere on your computer by adding their location to the system path:

- On Windows 8, 7, Windows Vista, or Windows XP, navigate through Start, Control Panel, System, Advanced System Settings, Environment Variables. Select the System Variable named "Path" then click the Edit button. Add the address of Java's **bin** sub-directory at the end of the list in the Variable Value field (for instance **C:\Java\bin;)** then click the OK button.

- On Linux, add the location of Java's **bin** sub-directory to the system path by editing the **.bashrc** file in your home directory. For instance, add **PATH=$PATH:/usr/Java/bin** then save the file.

To test the environment, open a prompt window then enter **java -version** and hit Return to see the interpreter's version number. Now, enter **javac -version** and hit Return to see the compiler's version number. Both numbers should match – in this case each is version number 1.8.0, and you're ready to start Java programming.

Paths that contain spaces must be enclosed within double quotes, such as **"C:\Program Files\Java\bin";**

Don't forget

If the **.bashrc** file is not immediately visible in your Linux home directory choose View, Show Hidden Files to reveal it.

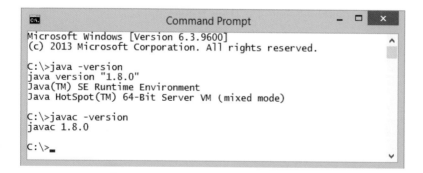

```
Microsoft Windows [Version 6.3.9600]
(c) 2013 Microsoft Corporation. All rights reserved.

C:\>java -version
java version "1.8.0"
Java(TM) SE Runtime Environment
Java HotSpot(TM) 64-Bit Server VM (mixed mode)

C:\>javac -version
javac 1.8.0

C:\>_
```

Beware

On older versions of Windows the JDK tools can be made globally available by editing the **autoexec.bat** file to add the location of Java's bin sub-directory at the end of the **SET PATH** line.

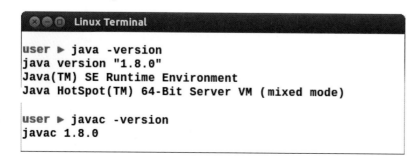

```
user ► java -version
java version "1.8.0"
Java(TM) SE Runtime Environment
Java HotSpot(TM) 64-Bit Server VM (mixed mode)

user ► javac -version
javac 1.8.0
```

Writing a first Java program

All Java programs start as text files that are later used to create "class" files, which are the actual runnable programs. This means that Java programs can be written in any plain text editor such as the Windows Notepad application.

Follow these steps to create a simple Java program that will output the traditional first program greeting:

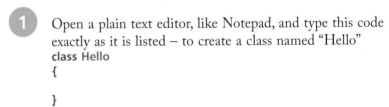

Hello.java

Beware

Java is a case-sensitive language where "Hello" and "hello" are distinctly different – traditionally, Java program names should always begin with an uppercase letter.

Don't forget

Java programs are always saved as their exact program name followed by the ".java" extension.

1 Open a plain text editor, like Notepad, and type this code exactly as it is listed – to create a class named "Hello"

```
class Hello
{

}
```

2 Between the curly brackets of the **Hello** class, insert this code – to create a "main" method for the **Hello** class

```
public static void main ( String[] args )
{

}
```

3 Between the curly brackets of the **main** method, insert this line of code – stating what the program will do

```
System.out.println( "Hello World!" ) ;
```

4 Save the file at any convenient location, but be sure to name it precisely as **Hello.java** – the complete program should now look like this:

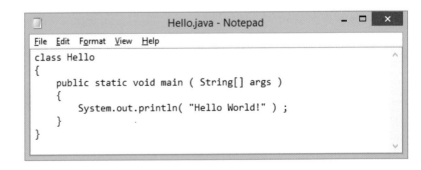

Hello.java - Notepad

File   Edit   Format   View   Help

```
class Hello
{
    public static void main ( String[] args )
    {
        System.out.println( "Hello World!" ) ;
    }
}
```

The separate parts of the program code on the opposite page can be examined individually to understand each part more clearly:

The Program Container

class Hello {   }

The program name is declared following the **class** keyword and followed by a pair of curly brackets. All of the program code that defines the **Hello** class will be contained within these curly brackets.

The Main Method

public static void main (String[] args) {   }

This fearsome-looking line is the standard code that is used to define the starting point of nearly all Java programs. It will be used in most examples throughout this book exactly as it appears above – so it may be useful to memorize it.

The code declares a method named "main" that will contain the actual program instructions within its curly brackets.

Keywords **public static void** precede the method name to define how the method may be used and are explained in detail later.

The code **(String[] args)** is useful when passing values to the method and is also fully explained later in this book.

The Statement

System.out.println("Hello World!") ;

Statements are actual instructions to perform program tasks and must always end with a semi-colon. A method may contain many statements inside its curly brackets to form a "statement block" defining a series of tasks to perform, but here a single statement instructs the program to output a line of text.

Turn to page 14 to discover how to compile and run this program.

All stand-alone Java programs must have a main method. Java applets are different and their format is explained later.

13

Create a MyJava directory in which to save all your Java program files.

Compiling & running programs

Before a Java program can run it must first be compiled into a **class** file by the Java compiler. This is located in Java's **bin** sub-directory and is an application named **javac**. The instructions on page 11 described how to add the **bin** sub-directory to the system path so that **javac** can be invoked from any system location.

Follow these steps to compile the program on the previous page:

1 Open a Command Prompt/Terminal window then navigate to the directory where you saved the **Hello.java** source code file

2 At the prompt, type **javac** followed by a space then the full name of the source code file **Hello.java** and hit Return

```
C:\>cd MyJava

C:\MyJava>javac Hello.java

C:\MyJava>_
```

If the **javac** compiler discovers errors in the code it will halt and display a helpful report indicating the nature of the error – see page 22 for Troubleshooting Problems.

If the **javac** compiler does not find any errors it will create a new file with the program name and the **.class** file extension.

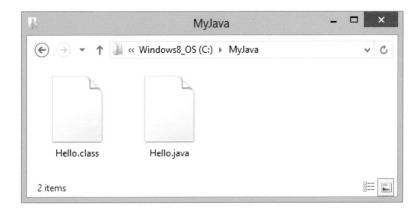

14

...cont'd

When the Java compiler completes compilation the Command Prompt/Terminal window focus returns to the prompt without any confirmation message – and the program is ready to run.

The Java program interpreter is an application named **java** that is located in Java's **bin** sub-directory – alongside the **javac** compiler. As this directory was previously added to the system path, on page 11, the **java** interpreter can be invoked from any location.

Follow these steps to run the program that was compiled using the procedure described on the page opposite:

1 Open a Command Prompt/Terminal window then navigate to the directory where the **Hello.class** program file is located

2 At the prompt, type **java** followed by a space then the program name **Hello** and hit Return

```
Command Prompt                    — ☐ ✕
C:\>cd MyJava

C:\MyJava>java Hello
Hello World!

C:\MyJava>_
```

The **Hello** program runs and executes the task defined in the statement within its main method – to output "Hello World!". Upon completion, focus returns to the prompt once more.

The process of compiling and running a Java program is typically combined in sequential steps, and is the same regardless of platform. The screenshot below illustrates the **Hello** program being compiled and run in combined steps on a Linux system:

Beware

Do not include the .class extension when running a program – only use the program name.

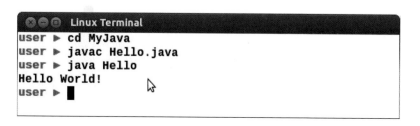

```
Linux Terminal
user ▶ cd MyJava
user ▶ javac Hello.java
user ▶ java Hello
Hello World!
user ▶ █
```

Creating a variable

In Java programming, a "variable" is simply a useful container in which a value may be stored for subsequent use by the program. The stored value may be changed (vary) as the program executes its instructions – hence the term "variable".

A variable is created by writing a variable "declaration" in the program, specifying the type of data that variable may contain and a given name for that variable. For example, the **String** data type can be specified to allow a variable named "message" to contain regular text with this declaration:

String message ;

Variable names are chosen by the programmer but must adhere to certain naming conventions. The variable name may only begin with a letter, dollar sign $, or the underscore character _ , and may subsequently have only letters, digits, dollar signs, or underscore characters. Names are case-sensitive, so "var" and "Var" are distinctly different names, and spaces are not allowed in names.

Variable names should also avoid the Java keywords, listed in the table below, as these have special meaning in the Java language:

abstract	default	goto	package	synchronized
assert	do	if	private	this
boolean	double	implements	protected	throw
break	else	import	public	throws
byte	enum	instanceof	return	transient
case	extends	int	short	true
catch	false	interface	static	try
char	final	long	strictfp	void
class	finally	native	String	volatile
const	float	new	super	while
continue	for	null	switch	

Beware

Each variable declaration must be terminated with a semi-colon character – like all other statements.

Hot tip

Strictly speaking, some words in this table are not actually keywords – **true**, **false**, and **null** are all literals, **String** is a special class name, **const** and **goto** are reserved words (currently unused). These are included in the table because they must also be avoided when naming variables.

...cont'd

As good practice, variables should be named with words or easily recognizable abbreviations, describing that variable's purpose. For example, "button1" or "btn1" to describe button number one. Lowercase letters are preferred for single-word names, such as "gear", and names that consist of multiple words should capitalize the first letter of each subsequent word, such as "gearRatio" – the so-called "camelCase" naming convention.

Once a variable has been declared, it may be assigned an initial value of the appropriate data type using the equals sign = , either in the declaration or later on in the program, then its value can be referenced at any time using the variable's name.

Follow these steps to create a program that declares a variable, which gets initialized in its declaration then changed later.

1 Start a new program named "FirstVariable", containing the standard main method
```
class FirstVariable
{
        public static void main ( String[] args ) {          }
}
```

JAVA

FirstVariable.java

2 Between the curly brackets of the main method, insert this code to create, intialize, and output a variable
```
String message = "Initial value" ;
System.out.println( message ) ;
```

3 Add these lines to modify and output the variable value
```
message = "Modified value" ;
System.out.println( message ) ;
```

Don't forget

4 Save the program as **FirstVariable.java** then compile and run the program

If you encounter problems compiling or running the program you can get help from Troubleshooting Problems on page 22.

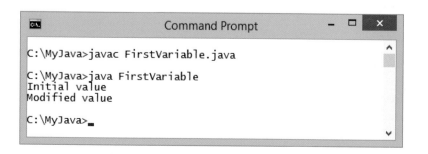

```
C:\MyJava>javac FirstVariable.java

C:\MyJava>java FirstVariable
Initial value
Modified value

C:\MyJava>_
```

Recognizing data types

The most frequently used data types in Java variable declarations are listed in this table along with a brief description:

Due to the irregularities of floating-point arithmetic the **float** data type should never be used for precise values, such as currency – see page 130 for details.

Data type:	Description:	Example:
char	A single Unicode character	'a'
String	Any number of Unicode characters	"my String"
int	An integer number, from -2.14 billion to +2.14 billion	1000
float	A floating-point number, with a decimal point	3.14159265f
boolean	A logical value of either true or false	true

Notice that **char** data values must always be surrounded by single quotes and **String** data values must always be surrounded by double quotes. Also remember that **float** data values must always have an "f" suffix to ensure they are treated as a **float** value.

In addition to the more common data types above, Java provides these specialized data types for use in exacting circumstances:

All data type keywords begin with a lowercase letter except **String** – which is a special class.

Data type:	Description:
byte	Integer number from -128 to +127
short	Integer number from -32,768 to +32,767
long	Positive or negative integer exceeding 2.14 billion
double	Extremely long floating-point number

Specialized data types are useful in advanced Java programs – the examples in this book mostly use the common data types described in the top table.

Follow these steps to create a Java program that creates, initializes, and outputs variables of all five common data types:

1 Start a new program named "DataTypes" containing the standard main method

```
class DataTypes
{
        public static void main ( String[] args ) {          }
}
```

DataTypes.java

2 Between the curly brackets of the main method, insert these declarations to create and intialize five variables

```
char letter = 'M' ;
String title = "Java in easy steps" ;
int number = 365 ;
float decimal = 98.6f ;
boolean result = true ;
```

3 Add these lines to output an appropriate text **String** concatenated to the value of each variable

```
System.out.println( "Intial is " + letter ) ;
System.out.println( "Book is " + title ) ;
System.out.println( "Days are " + number ) ;
System.out.println( "Temperature is " + decimal ) ;
System.out.println( "Answer is " + result ) ;
```

Hot tip

Notice how the + character is used here to join (concatenate) text strings and stored variable values.

4 Save the program as **DataTypes.java** then compile and run the program

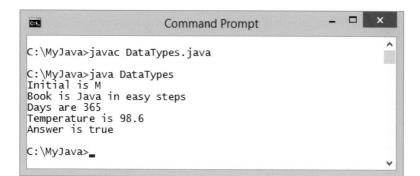

```
C:\MyJava>javac DataTypes.java

C:\MyJava>java DataTypes
Initial is M
Book is Java in easy steps
Days are 365
Temperature is 98.6
Answer is true

C:\MyJava>
```

Hot tip

The Java compiler will report an error if the program attempts to assign a value of the wrong data type to a variable – try changing the values in this example, then attempt to recompile the program to see the effect.

Creating constants

The "final" keyword is a modifier that can be used when declaring variables to prevent any subsequent changes to the values that are initially assigned to them. This is useful when storing a fixed value in a program to avoid it becoming altered accidentally.

Variables created to store fixed values in this way are known as "constants" and it is convention to name constants with all uppercase characters – to distinguish them from regular variables. Programs that attempt to change a constant value will not compile and the **javac** compiler will generate an error message.

Follow these steps to create a Java program featuring constants:

Constants.java

1 Start a new program named "Constants" containing the standard main method
```
class Constants
{
        public static void main ( String[] args ) {          }
}
```

2 Between the curly brackets of the main method, insert this code to create and intialize three integer constants
```
final int TOUCHDOWN = 6 ;
final int CONVERSION = 1 ;
final int FIELDGOAL = 3 ;
```

3 Now, declare four regular integer variables
```
int td , pat , fg , total ;
```

Hot tip

The * asterisk character is used here to multiply the constant values, and parentheses surround their addition for clarity.

4 Intialize the regular variables – using multiples of the constant values
```
td = 4 * TOUCHDOWN ;
pat = 3 * CONVERSION ;
fg = 2 * FIELDGOAL ;
total = ( td + pat + fg ) ;
```

5 Add this line to display the total score
```
System.out.println( "Score: " + total ) ;
```

6 Save the program as **Constants.java** then compile and run the program to see the output, Score: 33
(4 x 6 = 24, 3 x 1 = 3, 2 x 3 = 6, so 24 + 3 + 6 = 33)

Adding comments

When programming, in any language, it is good practice to add comments to program code to explain each particular section. This makes the code more easily understood by others, and by yourself when revisiting a piece of code after a period of absence.

In Java programming, comments can be added across multiple lines between /* and */ comment identifiers, or on a single line after a // comment identifier. Anything appearing between /* and */, or on a line after //, is completely ignored by the **javac** compiler.

When comments have been added to the **Constants.java** program, described opposite, the source code might look like this:

```
/*
        A program to demonstrate constant variables.
*/

class Constants
{
        public static void main( String args[] )
        {
                // Constant score values.
                final int TOUCHDOWN = 6 ;
                final int CONVERSION = 1 ;
                final int FIELDGOAL = 3 ;

                // Calculate points scored.
                int td , pat , fg , total ;
                td = 4 * TOUCHDOWN ;        // 4x6=24
                pat = 3 * CONVERSION ;      // 3x1= 3
                fg  = 2 * FIELDGOAL ;       // 2x3= 6
                total = ( td + pat + fg ) ; // 24+3+6=33

                // Output calculated total.
                System.out.println( "Score: " + total ) ;
        }
}
```

Saved with comments, the program compiles and runs as normal.

```
C:\MyJava>javac Constants.java

C:\MyJava>java Constants
Score: 33

C:\MyJava>_
```

Constants.java
(commented)

You can add a statement that attempts to change the value of a constant, then try to recompile the program to see the resulting error message.

Troubleshooting problems

Sometimes the **javac** compiler or **java** interpreter will complain about errors so it's useful to understand their cause and how to quickly resolve the problem. In order to demonstrate some common error reports, this code contains some deliberate errors:

Test.java

```
class test
{
        public static void main ( String[] args )
        {
                String text ;
                System.out.println( "Test " + text )
        }
}
```

A first attempt to compile **Test.java** throws up this error report:

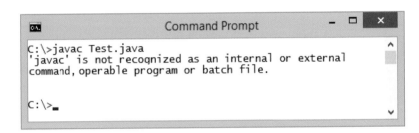

- Cause – the **javac** compiler cannot be found

- Solution – edit the system **PATH** variable, as described on page 11, or use its full path address to invoke the compiler

Hot tip

The path address must be enclosed within quotation marks if it contains any spaces, such as the path address "C:\Program Files\Java".

```
C:\>C:\Java\bin\javac Test.java
javac: file not found: Test.java
Usage: javac <options> <source files>
use -help for a list of possible options

C:\>_
```

- Cause – the file **Test.java** cannot be found

- Solution – navigate to the directory where the file is located, or use the full path address to the file in the command

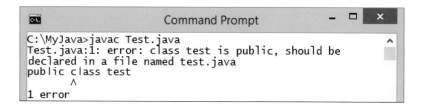

- Cause – the statement is not terminated correctly

- Solution – in the source code add a semi-colon at the end of the statement, then save the file to apply the change

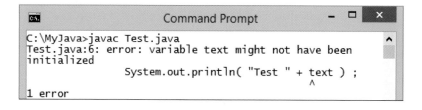

- Cause – the program name and class name do not match

- Solution – in the source code change the class name from **test** to **Test**, then save the file to apply the change

Beware

You must run the program from within its directory – you cannot use a path address as the java launcher requires a program name, not a file name.

- Cause – the variable **text** has no value

- Solution – in the variable declaration assign the variable a valid **String** value, for instance **= "success"**, then save the file

Summary

- Java is both a programming language and a runtime platform

- Java programs are written as plain text files with a **.java** extension

- The Java compiler **javac** creates compiled **.class** program files from original **.java** source code files

- The Java interpreter **java** executes compiled programs using an instance of the Java Virtual Machine

- The Java VM is available on many operating system platforms

- Adding Java's **bin** sub-directory to the system **PATH** variable allows the **javac** compiler to be invoked from anywhere

- Java is a case-sensitive language

- The standard **main** method is the entry point for Java programs

- The **System.out.println()** statement outputs text

- A Java program file name must exactly match its class name

- Java variables can only be named in accordance with specified naming conventions and must avoid the Java keywords

- In Java programming, each statement must be terminated by a semi-colon character

- The most common Java data types are **String, int, char, float** and **boolean**

- **String** values must be enclosed in double quotes, **char** values in single quotes, and **float** values must have an "f" suffix

- The **final** keyword can be used to create a constant variable

- Comments can be added to Java source code between /* and */, on one or more lines, or after // on a single line

- Error reports identify compiler and runtime problems

2 Performing operations

This chapter demonstrates the various operators that are used to create expressions in Java programs.

Doing arithmetic

Arithmetical operators, listed in the table below, are used to create expressions in Java programs that return a single resulting value. For example, the expression **4 * 2** returns the value **8**:

Operator:	Operation:
+	Addition (and concatenates String values)
-	Subtraction
*	Multiplication
/	Division
%	Modulus
++	Increment
--	Decrement

The increment operator **++** , and decrement operator **--** , return the result of modifying a single given operand by a value of one. For example, **4++** returns the value **5**, and **4--** returns the value **3**.

All other arithmetic operators return the result of an operation performed on two given operands, and act as you would expect. For example, the expression **5 + 2** returns **7**.

The modulus operator divides the first operand by the second operand and returns the remainder of the operation. For example, **32 % 5** returns **2** – five divides into 32 six times, with 2 remainder.

The operation performed by the addition operator + depends on the type of its given operands. Where both operands are numeric values it will return the total sum value of those numbers, but where the operands are **String** values it will return a single concatenated **String** – combining the text in each **String** operand. For example, **"Java " + "Arithmetic"** returns **"Java Arithmetic"**.

Hot tip

Increment and decrement operators are typically used to count the iterations in the for loop constructs, introduced on page 50.

Follow these steps to create a Java program featuring some of the arithmetic operators.

1 Start a new program named "Arithmetic" containing the standard main method

```
class Arithmetic
{
        public static void main( String[] args ) {          }
}
```

Arithmetic.java

2 Between the curly brackets of the main method, declare and initialize three integer variables

```
int num = 100 ;
int factor = 20 ;
int sum = 0 ;
```

3 Add these lines to perform addition and subtraction operations, displaying each returned total

```
sum = num + factor ;   // 100 + 20
System.out.println( "Addition sum: " + sum ) ;
sum = num - factor ;    // 100 - 20
System.out.println( "Subtraction sum: " + sum ) ;
```

4 Now, add these lines to perform multiplication and division operations, displaying each returned total

```
sum = num * factor ;    // 100 x 20
System.out.println( "Multiplication sum: " + sum ) ;

sum = num / factor ;     // 100 ÷ 20
System.out.println( "Division sum: " + sum ) ;
```

5 Save the program as **Arithmetic.java** then compile and run the program

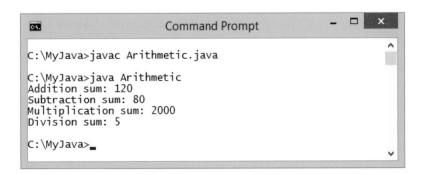

Don't forget

The statement that outputs each result uses the + operator to concatenate a text string and the integer sum into a single string.

Assigning values

Assignment operators, listed in the table below, are used to assign the result of an expression. All except the simple = operator are the shorthand form of a longer equivalent expression:

Operator:	Example:	Equivalent:
=	a = b	a = b
+=	a += b	a = a + b
-=	a -= b	a = a - b
*=	a *= b	a = a * b
/=	a /= b	a = a / b
%=	a %= b	a = a % b

It is important to regard the = operator to mean "assign", rather than "equals", to avoid confusion with the == equality operator.

In the example **a = b** the value stored in the variable named **b** is assigned to the variable named **a**, so that value becomes the new value stored in **a** – replacing any value it previously contained.

The **+=** operator is useful to add a value onto an existing value stored in a variable – keeping a "running total".

The example **a += b** first calculates the sum total of the values stored in the variables named **a** and **b**, then assigns the resulting total to variable **a**. A program might then contain a further assignment **a += c** that calculates the total stored in variables named **a** and **c**, then assigns that new total to variable **a** – adding the value of **c** to the value it previously contained.

All the other assignment operators work in the same way by first performing the arithmetical calculation on the two stored values, then assigning the result to the first variable – to become its new stored value.

Don't forget

The == equality operator compares values and is fully explained on page 30.

Follow these steps to create a Java program featuring various assignment operators:

1 Start a new program named "Assignment" containing the standard main method

```
class Assignment
{
        public static void main( String[] args ) {          }
}
```

Assignment.java

2 Between the curly brackets of the main method, insert this code to add and assign a text **String** value

```
String txt = "Fantastic " ;
String lang = "Java" ;
txt += lang ;    // Assign concatenated String
System.out.println( "Add & Assign Strings: " + txt ) ;
```

3 Insert these lines to add and assign an integer

```
int sum = 10 ;
int num = 20 ;
sum += num ; // Assign result ( 10 + 20 = 30 )
System.out.println( "Add & Assign Integers: " + sum ) ;
```

4 Insert these lines to multiply and assign an integer

```
int factor = 5 ;
sum *= factor ; // Assign result ( 30 x 5 = 150 )
System.out.println( "Multiplication sum: " + sum ) ;
```

5 Insert these lines to divide and assign an integer

```
sum /= factor ; // Assign result ( 150 ÷ 5 = 30 )
System.out.println( "Division sum: " + sum ) ;
```

6 Save the program as **Assignment.java** then compile and run the program

Assignment of the wrong data type to a variable will cause an error.

```
Command Prompt                              –  □  ×

C:\MyJava>javac Assignment.java

C:\MyJava>java Assignment
Add & Assign Strings: Fantastic Java
Add & Assign Integers: 30
Multiplication sum: 150
Division sum: 30
```

Comparing values

Comparison operators, listed in the table below, are used to compare two values in an expression and return a single Boolean value of **true** or **false** – describing the result of that comparison:

Operator:	Comparison:
==	Equality
!=	Inequality
>	Greater than
>=	Greater than, or equal to
<	Less than
<=	Less than, or equal to

The == equality operator compares two operands and will return **true** if both are exactly equal in value. If both are the same number they are equal, or if both are **String** values containing the same characters in the same order they are equal. Boolean operands that are both **true**, or that are both **false**, are equal.

Conversely, the != inequality operator returns **true** if two operands are not equal – applying the same rules as the equality operator.

Equality and inequality operators are useful in testing the state of two variables to perform "conditional branching" of a program – proceeding in different directions according to the condition.

The > "greater than" operator compares two operands and will return **true** if the first is greater in value than the second.

The < "less than" operator makes the same comparison but returns true if the first operand is less in value than the second.

Adding the = assignment operator after the > "greater than" operator, or after the < "less than" operator, makes it also return **true** when the two operands are exactly equal in value.

Hot tip

The < less than operator is typically used to test a counter value in a loop – an example of this can be found on page 50.

...cont'd

Follow these steps to create a Java program featuring various comparison operators:

1 Start a new program named "Comparison" containing the standard main method

```
class Comparison
{
        public static void main( String[] args ) {          }
}
```

Comparison.java

2 Between the curly brackets of the main method, insert this code to compare two text **String** values for equality

```
String txt = "Fantastic " ;
String lang = "Java" ;
boolean state = ( txt == lang ) ; // Assign test result
System.out.println( "String Equality Test: " + state ) ;
```

3 Add these lines to compare for inequality

```
state = ( txt != lang ) ;           // Assign result
System.out.println( "String Inequality Test: " + state ) ;
```

Hot tip

Notice how an expression can be contained in parentheses for better readability.

4 Now, add these lines to compare two integer values

```
int dozen = 12 ;
int score = 20 ;
state = ( dozen > score ) ;         // Assign result
System.out.println( "Greater Than Test : " + state ) ;
```

31

5 Add two more lines to compare the integers once more

```
state = ( dozen < score ) ;         // Assign result
System.out.println( "Less Than Test: " + state ) ;
```

6 Save the program as **Comparison.java** then compile and run the program

Don't forget

Here it's untrue (**false**) that the **String** values are equal, but it is **true** that they are unequal.

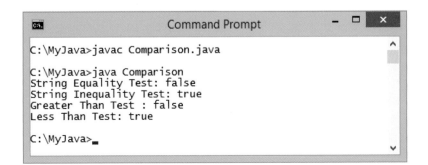

```
C:\MyJava>javac Comparison.java

C:\MyJava>java Comparison
String Equality Test: false
String Inequality Test: true
Greater Than Test : false
Less Than Test: true

C:\MyJava>_
```

Assessing logic

Logical operators, listed in the table below, are used to combine multiple expressions that each return a Boolean value – into a complex expression that returns a single Boolean value:

Operator:	Operation:
&&	Logical AND
||	Logical OR
!	Logical NOT

Logical operators are used with operands that have the Boolean values of **true** or **false**, or values that can convert to **true** or **false**.

The logical **&&** AND operator will evaluate two operands and return **true** only if both operands are themselves **true**. Otherwise the logical **&&** operator will return **false**. This evaluation can be used in conditional branching where a program will only perform a certain action when two tested conditions are both true.

Unlike the logical **&&** operator, that needs two operands to be **true**, the logical **||** OR operator will evaluate its two operands and return **true** if either one of the operands is **true** – it will only return **false** when neither operand is **true**. This is useful in Java programming to perform a certain action when either one of two test conditions has been met.

The logical **!** NOT operator is a "unary" operator, that is used before a single operand. It returns the inverse Boolean value of the given operand – reversing **true** to **false**, and **false** to **true**. It's useful in Java programs to toggle the value of a variable in successive loop iterations with a statement like **goState=!goState**. This ensures that on each pass of the loop the value is changed, like flicking a light switch on and off.

Follow these steps to create a Java program featuring the three logical operators:

1 Start a new program named "Logic" containing the standard main method

```
class Logic
{
        public static void main( String[] args ) {          }
}
```

Logic.java

2 Between the curly brackets of the main method, insert this code to declare and initialize two Boolean variables

```
boolean yes = true ;
boolean no = false ;
```

3 Add these lines to test if both two conditions are true

```
System.out.println( "Both YesYes True: " + ( yes && yes ) ) ;
System.out.println( "Both YesNo True: " + ( yes && no ) ) ;
```

4 Add these lines to test if either of two conditions is true

```
System.out.println( "Either YesYes True: " + ( yes || yes ) ) ;
System.out.println( "Either YesNo True: " + ( yes || no ) ) ;
System.out.println( "Either NoNo True: " + ( no || no ) ) ;
```

5 Add two more lines to show an original and inverse value

```
System.out.println( "Original Yes Value: " + yes ) ;
System.out.println( "Inverse Yes Value: " + !yes ) ;
```

6 Save the program as **Logic.java** then compile and run the program

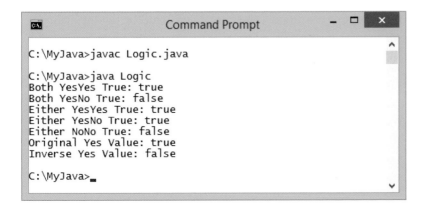

```
C:\MyJava>javac Logic.java

C:\MyJava>java Logic
Both YesYes True: true
Both YesNo True: false
Either YesYes True: true
Either YesNo True: true
Either NoNo True: false
Original Yes Value: true
Inverse Yes Value: false

C:\MyJava>_
```

Hot tip

The **boolean** data type is named after mathematician George Boole – the inventor of Boolean algebra.

Examining conditions

Possibly the all-time favorite operator of the Java programmer is the **?** : conditional operator that makes a powerful statement very concisely. Its unusual syntax can seem tricky to understand at first but it is well worth getting to know this useful operator.

The conditional operator first evaluates an expression for a **true** or **false** value then returns one of two given operands depending on the result of the evaluation. Its syntax looks like this:

(*boolean-expression*) **?** *if-true-return-this* : *if-false-return-this* ;

Each specified operand alternative allows the progam to progress according to the Boolean value returned by the tested expression. For instance, the alternatives might return a **String** value:

status = (quit == true) ? "Done!" : "Continuing..." ;

In this case, when the **quit** variable is **true** the conditional operator assigns the value of its first operand to the **status** variable, otherwise it assigns its second operand value instead.

A shorthand available when coding Java programs allows expressions to optionally omit **== true** when evaluating a simple Boolean value, so the example above can be written simply as:

status = (quit) ? "Done!" : "Continuing..." ;

The conditional operator can return values of any data type and employ any valid test expression. For instance, the expression might use the greater than **>** operator to evaluate two numeric values then return a Boolean value depending on the result:

busted = (speed > speedLimit) ? true : false ;

Similarly, the conditional operator might employ the inequality **!=** operator to evaluate a **String** value then return a numeric value depending on the result:

bodyTemperature = (scale != "Celsius") ? 98.6 : 37.0 ;

Hot tip

The conditional operator is also known as the "ternary" operator.

...cont'd

Follow these steps to create a Java program featuring the conditional operator:

1 Start a new program named "Condition" containing the standard main method

```
class Condition
{
        public static void main( String[] args ) {          }
}
```

Condition.java

2 Between the curly brackets of the main method, insert this code to declare and initialize two integer variables

```
int num1 = 1357 ;
int num2 = 2468 ;
```

3 Declare a further variable to store a test result **String**

```
String result ;
```

4 Add these lines to determine whether the first integer value is an odd or even number

```
result = ( num1 % 2 != 0 ) ? "Odd" : "Even" ;
System.out.println( num1 + " is " + result ) ;
```

5 Now, add these lines to determine whether the second integer value is an odd or even number

```
result = ( num2 % 2 != 0 ) ? "Odd" : "Even" ;
System.out.println( num2 + " is " + result ) ;
```

6 Save the program as **Condition.java** then compile and run the program

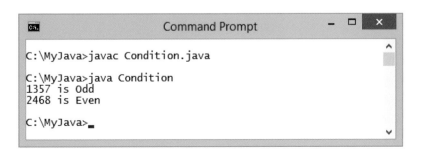

```
C:\MyJava>javac Condition.java

C:\MyJava>java Condition
1357 is Odd
2468 is Even

C:\MyJava>_
```

Here, the expression evaluates as true when there is any remainder.

Setting precedence

Complex expressions, which contain multiple operators and operands, can be ambiguous unless the order in which the operations should be executed is clear. This lack of clarity can easily cause different results to be implied by the same expression. For example, consider this complex expression:

num = 8 + 4 * 2 ;

Working left-to-right **8 + 4 = 12**, and **12 * 2 = 24**, so **num = 24**. But working right-to-left **2 * 4 = 8**, and **8 + 8 = 16**, so **num = 16**.

The Java programmer can explicitly specify which operation should be executed first by adding parentheses to signify which operator has precedence. In this case **(8 + 4) * 2** ensures that the addition is performed before the multiplication – so the result is 24, not 16. Conversely, **8 + (4 * 2)** performs the multiplication first – so the result is 16, not 24.

Where parentheses do not explicitly specify operator precedence, Java follows the default precedence order listed in the table below, from first at the top to last at the bottom:

Hot tip

Operators of equal precedence are handled in the order they appear in the expression – from left to right.

Operator:	Description:
++ -- !	Increment, Decrement, Logical NOT
* / %	Multiplication, Division, Modulus
+ -	Addition, Subtraction
> >= < <=	Greater than, Greater than or equal to Less than, Less than or equal to
== !=	Equality, Inequality
&&	Logical AND
||	Logical OR
? :	Conditional
= += -= *= /= %=	Assignment

...cont'd

Follow these steps to create a Java program featuring various operator precedence:

1 Start a new program named "Precedence" containing the standard main method

```
class Precedence
{
        public static void main( String[] args ) {          }
}
```

Precedence.java

2 Between the curly brackets of the main method, insert this code to declare and initialize an integer variable with the result of an expression using default precedence

```
int sum = 32 - 8 + 16 * 2 ;        // 16 x 2 = 32, + 24 = 56
System.out.println( "Default order: " + sum ) ;
```

3 Add these lines to assign the result of the same expression to the integer variable – giving addition and subtraction precedence over multiplication

```
sum = ( 32 - 8 + 16 ) * 2 ;        // 24 + 16 = 40, x 2 = 80
System.out.println( "Specified order: " + sum ) ;
```

4 Add these lines to assign the integer variable the result of the same expression where the operation precedence order is first addition, then subtraction, and then multiplication

```
sum = ( 32 - (8 + 16) ) * 2 ;      // 32 - 24 = 8, * 2 = 16
System.out.println( "Nested specific order: " + sum ) ;
```

5 Save the program as **Precedence.java** then compile and run the program

Don't forget

Where expressions have multiple nested parentheses the innermost takes precedence.

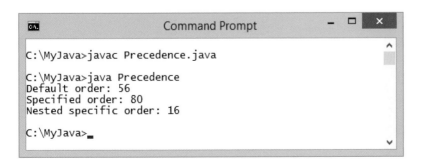

```
Command Prompt                    –  □  ×

C:\MyJava>javac Precedence.java

C:\MyJava>java Precedence
Default order: 56
Specified order: 80
Nested specific order: 16

C:\MyJava>_
```

Escaping literals

The numerical and text values in Java programs are known as "literals" – they represent nothing but are, literally, what you see.

Literals are normally detached from the keywords of the Java language but where double quotes, or single quotes, are required within a **String** value it is necessary to indicate that the quote character is to be treated literally to avoid prematurely terminating the **String**. This is easily achieved by immediately prefixing each nested quote character with the \ escape operator. For example, including a quote within a **String** variable like this:

String quote = " \"Fortune favors the brave.\" said Virgil ";

Additionally, the \ escape operator offers a variety of useful escape sequences for simple output formatting:

Escape:	Description:
\n	Newline
\t	Tab
\b	Backspace
\r	Carriage return
\f	Formfeed
\\	Backslash
\'	Single quote mark
\"	Double quote mark

The \n newline escape sequence is frequently used within long **String** values to display the output on multiple lines. Similarly, the \t tab escape sequence is frequently used to display the output in columns. Using a combination of \n newline and \t tab escape sequences allows the output to be formatted in both rows and columns – to resemble a table.

Hot tip

Single quotes can be nested within double quotes as an alternative to escaping quote characters.

Follow these steps to create a Java program using escape sequences to format the output:

1 Start a new program named "Escape" containing the standard main method

```
class Escape
{
        public static void main( String[] args ) {          }
}
```

Escape.java

2 Between the curly brackets of the main method, insert this code to build a **String** containing a formatted table title and column headings

```
String header = "\n\tNEW YORK 3-DAY FORECAST:\n" ;
header += "\n\tDay\t\tHigh\tLow\tConditions\n" ;
header += "\t---\t\t----\t---\t----------\n" ;
```

3 Add these lines to build a **String** containing formatted table cell data

```
String forecast = "\tSunday\t\t68F\t48F\tSunny\n" ;
forecast += "\tMonday\t\t69F\t57F\tSunny\n" ;
forecast += "\tTuesday\t\t71F\t50F\tCloudy\n" ;
```

4 Now, add this line to output both formatted **String** values

```
System.out.print( header + forecast ) ;
```

5 Save the program as **Escape.java** then compile and run the program

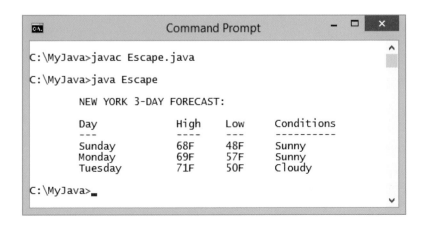

In this case, escape sequences add newlines so the **print()** method is used here – rather than the **println()** method that automatically adds a newline after output.

Working with bits

In addition to the regular operators, described throughout this chapter, Java provides special operators for binary arithmetic. These are less commonly used than other operators but are briefly discussed here to simply provide an awareness of their existence.

The Java "bitwise" operators can be used with the **int** integer data type to manipulate the bits of the binary representation of a value. This requires an understanding of binary numbering, where eight bits in a byte represent decimal values zero to 255. For example, 53 is binary **00110101** (0x128,0x64,1x32,1x16,0x8,1x4,0x2,1x1).

Binary addition operations are performed like decimal arithmetic:

$$
\begin{array}{rcl}
53 & = & 00110101 \\
+\ \underline{7} & = & \underline{00000111} \\
\underline{60} & = & \underline{00111100}
\end{array}
$$

The bitwise operators, listed below, allow more specialized operations to be performed in binary arithemetic:

Operator:	Operation:	Example:	Result:
&	AND	a & b	1 if both bits are 1
|	OR	a | b	1 if either bit is 1
^	XOR	a ^ b	1 if both bits differ
~	NOT	~a	Inverts the bits
<<	Left shift	n << p	Moves n bits p left
>>	Right shift	n >> p	Moves n bits p right

For example, using the bitwise **&** operator in binary arithmetic:

$$
\begin{array}{rcl}
53 & = & 00110101 \\
\&\ \underline{7} & = & \underline{00000111} \\
\underline{5} & = & \underline{00000101}
\end{array}
$$

Beware

Don't confuse the logical AND operator **&&** with the bitwise **&** operator, or the logical OR operator **||** with the bitwise **|** operator.

...cont'd

A common use of bitwise operators combines several values in a single variable for efficiency. For instance, a program with several "flag" **int** variables, with values of 1 or 0 (representing on and off states), would normally require 8 bits of memory each. These values only really require a single bit, however, so up to eight flags can be combined in a single **int** variable – using one bit per flag. The status of each flag can be retrieved with bitwise operations:

1 Start a new program named "Bitwise" containing the standard main method
```
class Bitwise
{
        public static void main( String[] args ) {          }
}
```

Bitwise.java

2 Between the curly brackets of the main method, insert this code to declare and initialize an integer variable with a value representing the total status of up to eight flags
```
int fs = 53 ;     // Combined flag status of 00110101
```

3 Add these lines to retrieve the status of each flag
```
System.out.println("Flag 1: "+(( (fs&1)>0) ? "ON" : "off"));
System.out.println("Flag 2: "+(( (fs&2)>0) ? "ON" : "off"));
System.out.println("Flag 3: "+(( (fs&4)>0) ? "ON" : "off"));
System.out.println("Flag 4: "+(( (fs&8)>0) ? "ON" : "off"));
System.out.println("Flag 5: "+(( (fs&16)>0)? "ON" : "off"));
System.out.println("Flag 6: "+(( (fs&32)>0)? "ON" : "off"));
System.out.println("Flag 7: "+(( (fs&64)>0)? "ON" : "off"));
System.out.println("Flag 8: "+(( (fs&128)>0)?"ON": "off"));
```

4 Save the program as **Bitwise.java** then compile and run the program

```
C:\MyJava>javac Bitwise.java

C:\MyJava>java Bitwise
Flag 1: ON
Flag 2: off
Flag 3: ON
Flag 4: off
Flag 5: ON
Flag 6: ON
Flag 7: off
Flag 8: off
```
Command Prompt

Here, the bitwise **&** operation returns one or zero to determine each flag's status.

Summary

- Arithmetical operators can form expressions with two operands for addition +, subtraction -, multiplication *, division /, or modulus %

- Increment ++ and decrement -- operators modify a single operand by a value of one

- The assignment = operator can be combined with an arithmetical operator to perform an arithmetical calculation then assign its result

- Comparison operators can form expressions comparing two operands for equality ==, inequality !=, greater >, or lesser < values

- The assignment = operator can be combined with the greater than > or lesser than < operator to also return **true** when equal

- Logical && and || operators form expressions evaluating two operands to return a Boolean value of either **true** or **false**

- The logical ! operator returns the inverse Boolean value of a single operand

- A conditional ? : operator evaluates a given Boolean expression and returns one of two operands depending on its result

- Expressions evaluating a Boolean expression for a **true** value may optionally omit == **true**

- It is important to explicitly set operator precedence in complex expressions by adding parentheses ( )

- The backslash escape \ operator can be used to prefix quote characters within **String** values to prevent syntax errors

- Escape sequences \n newline and \t tab provide simple output formatting

- Bitwise operators can be useful to perform binary arithmetic in specialized situations

3 Making statements

This chapter demonstrates the various keywords that are used to create branching in Java programs.

Branching with if

The **if** keyword performs a conditional test to evaluate an expression for a Boolean value. A statement following the expression will only be executed when the evaluation is **true**, otherwise the program proceeds on to subsequent code – pursuing the next "branch". The **if** statement syntax looks like this:

if (*test-expression* **)** *code-to-be-executed-when-true* **;**

The code to be executed can contain multiple statements if they are enclosed within curly brackets to form a "statement block".

If.java

1 Start a new program named "If" containing the standard main method

```
class If
{
        public static void main ( String[] args) {          }
}
```

2 Between the curly brackets of the main method, insert this simple conditional test that executes a single statement when one number is greater than another

```
if ( 5 > 1 ) System.out.println( "Five is greater than one." ) ;
```

3 Add a second conditional test, which executes an entire statement block when one number is less than another

```
if ( 2 < 4 )
{
        System.out.println( "Two is less than four." ) ;
        System.out.println( "Test succeeded." ) ;
}
```

4 Save the program as **If.java** then compile and run the program to see all statements get executed – because both tests evaluate as **true** in this case

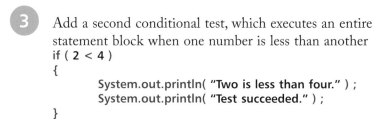

```
C:\MyJava>javac If.java

C:\MyJava>java If
Five is greater than one.
Two is less than four.
Test succeeded.

C:\MyJava>_
```

Hot tip

Expressions can utilize the **true** and **false** keywords. The test expression **(2 < 4)** is shorthand for **(2 < 4 == true)**.

44

A conditional test can also evaluate a complex expression to test multiple conditions for a Boolean value. Parentheses enclose each test condition to establish precedence – so they get evaluated first. The Boolean **&&** AND operator ensures the complex expression will only return **true** when both tested conditions are true:

if ((*test-condition-1*) **&&** (*test-condition-2*)) *execute-this-code* ;

The Boolean **||** OR operator ensures a complex expression will only return **true** when either one of the tested conditions is true:

if ((*test-condition-1*) **||** (*test-condition-2*)) *execute-this-code* ;

A combination of these can form longer complex expressions.

Hot tip

The range can be extended to include the upper and lower limits using the **>=** and **<=** operators.

5   Inside the main method of **If.java** insert this line to declare and initialize an integer variable named **num**
```
int num = 8 ;
```

6   Add a third conditional test that executes a statement when the value of the **num** variable is within a specified range, or when it's exactly equal to a specified value
```
if ( ( ( num > 5 ) && ( num < 10 ) ) || ( num == 12 ) )
System.out.println( "Number is 6-9 inclusive, or 12" ) ;
```

45

7   Recompile the program and run it once more to see the statement after the complex expression get executed

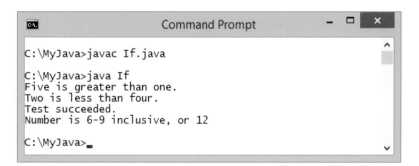

```
C:\MyJava>javac If.java

C:\MyJava>java If
Five is greater than one.
Two is less than four.
Test succeeded.
Number is 6-9 inclusive, or 12

C:\MyJava>
```

Don't forget

The complex expression uses the **==** equality operator to specify an exact match, not the **=** assignment operator.

8   Change the value assigned to the **num** variable so it is neither within the specified range 6-9, nor exactly 12. Recompile the program and run it again to now see the statement after the complex expression is not executed

Branching alternatives

The **else** keyword is used in conjunction with the **if** keyword to create **if else** statements that provide alternative branches for a program to pursue – according to the evaluation of a tested expression. In its simplest form this merely nominates an alternative statement for execution when the test fails:

if (*test-expression* **)**

        code-to-be-executed-when-true ;

else

        code-to-be-executed-when-false ;

Each alternative branch may be a single statement or a statement block of multiple statements – enclosed within curly brackets.

More powerful **if else** statements can be constructed that evaluate a test expression for each alternative branch. These employ nested **if** statements after each **else** keyword to specify each further test. When the program discovers an expression that evaluates as **true** it executes the statements associated with just that test then exits the **if else** statement without exploring any further branches:

Beware

Notice that the first statement is terminated with a semicolon, as usual, before the else keyword.

Else.java

1. Start a new program named "Else" containing the standard main method
```
class Else
{
        public static void main ( String[] args ) {          }
}
```

2. Inside the main method, insert this line to declare and initialize an integer variable named **hrs**
```
int hrs = 11 ;
```

3. Insert this simple conditional test, which executes a single statement when the value of the **hrs** variable is below 13
```
if ( hrs < 13 )
{
        System.out.println( "Good morning: " + hrs ) ;
}
```

4. Save the program as **Else.java** then compile and run the program to see the statement get executed

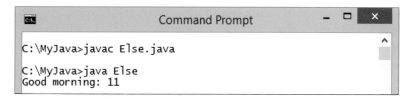

```
C:\MyJava>javac Else.java

C:\MyJava>java Else
Good morning: 11
```

5 Change the value assigned to the **hrs** variable to 15 then add this alternative branch right after the **if** statement

```
else if ( hrs < 18 )
{
        System.out.println( "Good afternoon: " + hrs ) ;
}
```

6 Save the changes, recompile, and run the program again to see just the alternative statement get executed

```
C:\MyJava>javac Else.java

C:\MyJava>java Else
Good afternoon: 15
```

It is sometimes desirable to provide a final **else** branch, without a nested **if** statement, to specify a "default" statement to be executed when no tested expression evaluates as **true**:

7 Change the value assigned to the **hrs** variable to 21, then add this default branch to the end of the **if else** statement

```
else System.out.println( "Good evening: " + hrs ) ;
```

8 Save the changes, recompile, and run the program once more to see just the default statement get executed

Conditional branching is the fundamental process by which computer programs proceed.

```
C:\MyJava>javac Else.java

C:\MyJava>java Else
Good evening: 21

C:\MyJava>
```

Switching branches

Lengthy **if else** statements, which offer many conditional branches for a program to pursue, can become unwieldy. Where the test expressions repeatedly evaluate the same variable value a more elegant solution is often provided by a **switch** statement.

The syntax of a typical switch statement block looks like this:

```
switch ( test-variable )
{
        case value-1 : code-to-be-executed-when-true ; break ;
        case value-2 : code-to-be-executed-when-true ; break ;
        case value-3 : code-to-be-executed-when-true ; break ;
        default : code-to-be-executed-when-false ;
}
```

The **switch** statement works in an unusual way. It takes a specified variable then seeks to match its assigned value from among a number of **case** options. Statements associated with the option whose value matches are then executed.

Optionally, a **switch** statement can include a final option using the **default** keyword to specify statements to execute when no case options match the value assigned to the specified variable.

Each option begins with the **case** keyword and a value to match. This is followed by a : colon character and the statements, if any, to be executed when the match is made.

It is important to recognize that the statement, or statement block, associated with each **case** option must be terminated by the **break** keyword. Otherwise the program will continue to execute the statements of other **case** options after the matched option. Sometimes this is desirable to specify a number of **case** options that should each execute the same statements if matched. For example, one statement for each block of three options like this:

```
switch ( test-variable )
{
        case value-1 : case value-2 : case value-3 :
                code-A-to-be-executed-when-true ; break ;

        case value-4 : case value-5 : case value-6 :
                code-B-to-be-executed-when-true ; break ;
}
```

Beware

Missing break keywords are not syntax errors – ensure that all intended breaks are present in switch blocks to avoid unexpected results.

...cont'd

1 Start a new program named "Switch" containing the standard main method

```
class Switch
{
        public static void main ( String[] args ) {          }
}
```

JAVA
Switch.java

2 Inside the main method, declare and initialize three integer variables

```
int month = 2, year = 2016, num = 31 ;
```

3 Add a switch statement block to test the value assigned to the **month** variable

```
switch ( month )
{

}
```

Hot tip

Notice how all three integer variables are declared and initialized inline here using convenient shorthand.

4 Inside the switch block, insert **case** options assigning a new value to the **num** variable for months 4, 6, 9 and 11

```
case 4 : case 6 : case 9 : case 11 : num = 30 ; break ;
```

5 Insert a **case** option assigning a new value to the **num** variable for month 2, according to the **year** value

```
case 2 : num = ( year % 4 == 0 ) ? 29 : 28 ; break ;
```

6 After the switch block, at the end of the main method, add this line to output all three integer values

```
System.out.println( month+"/"+year+": "+num+"days" ) ;
```

Don't forget

The conditional operator is used to good effect in step 5. You can check back to page 34 to be reminded how it works.

7 Save the program as **Switch.java** then compile and run the program to see the output

```
C:\MyJava>javac Switch.java

C:\MyJava>java Switch
2/2016: 29days

C:\MyJava>
```

Looping for

A loop is a block of code that repeatedly executes the statements it contains until a tested condition is met – then the loop ends and the program proceeds on to its next task.

The most frequently used loop structure in Java programming employs the **for** keyword and has this syntax:

for (*initializer* ; *test-expression* ; *updater*)
{
       statements-to-be-executed-on-each-iteration ;
}

The parentheses after the **for** keyword must contain three controls that establish the performance of the loop:

- **Initializer** – assigns an initial value to a counter variable, which will keep count of the number of iterations made by this loop. The variable for this purpose may be declared here and it is traditionally a "trivial" integer variable named **i**.

- **Test expression** – evaluated at the start of each iteration of the loop for a Boolean **true** value. When the evaluation returns **true** the iteration proceeds but when it returns **false** the loop is immediately terminated, without completing that iteration.

- **Updater** – changes the current value of the counter variable, started by the initializer, keeping the running total of the number of iterations made by this loop. Typically, this will use **i++** for counting up, or **i--** for counting down.

The code executed on each iteration of the loop can be a single statement, a statement block, or even another "nested" loop.

Every loop must, at some point, enable the test expression to return **false** – otherwise an infinite loop is created that will relentlessly execute its statements. Commonly, the test expression will evaluate the current value of the counter variable to perform a specified number of iterations. For example, with a counter **i** initialized at one and incremented by one on each iteration, a test expression of **i < 11** becomes false after 10 iterations – so that loop will execute its statements 10 times before the loop ends.

Hot tip

The updater is often referred to as the "incrementer" as it more often increments, rather than decrements, the counter variable.

1 Start a new program named "For" containing the standard main method

```
class For
{
        public static void main ( String[] args ) {          }
}
```

For.java

2 Inside the main method, declare and initialize an integer variable to count the total overall number of iterations

```
int num = 0 ;
```

3 Add a **for** loop to perform three iterations and display the current value of its counter variable **i** on each iteration

```
for ( int i = 1 ; i < 4 ; i++ )
{
        System.out.println( "Outer Loop i=" + i ) ;
}
```

4 Inside the **for** loop block insert a nested **for** loop to also perform three iterations, displaying the current value of its counter variable **j** and total overall number of iterations

```
for ( int j = 1 ; j < 4 ; j++ )
{
        System.out.print( "\tInner Loop j=" + j ) ;
        System.out.println( "\t\tTotal num="+ (++num) ) ;
}
```

5 Save the program as **For.java** then compile and run the program to see the output

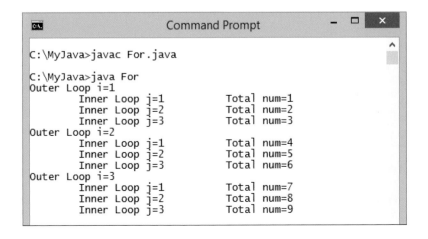

```
C:\MyJava>javac For.java

C:\MyJava>java For
Outer Loop i=1
        Inner Loop j=1          Total num=1
        Inner Loop j=2          Total num=2
        Inner Loop j=3          Total num=3
Outer Loop i=2
        Inner Loop j=1          Total num=4
        Inner Loop j=2          Total num=5
        Inner Loop j=3          Total num=6
Outer Loop i=3
        Inner Loop j=1          Total num=7
        Inner Loop j=2          Total num=8
        Inner Loop j=3          Total num=9
```

Beware

The increment **++** and decrement **--** operators can prefix a variable, to change its value immediately, or postfix the variable – so its value becomes changed when next referenced. Try changing the increment operators in this example to **++i** and **++j** to see the difference.

Looping while true

An alternative loop structure to that of the **for** loop, described on the previous page, employs the **while** keyword and has this syntax:

while (*test-expression* **)**
{

    statements-to-be-executed-on-each-iteration **;**

}

Like the **for** loop, a **while** loop repeatedly executes the statements it contains until a tested condition is met – then the loop ends and the program proceeds on to its next task.

Unlike the **for** loop, the parentheses after the **while** keyword do not contain an initializer or updater for an iteration counter variable. This means that the test expression must evaluate some value that gets changed in the loop statements as the loop proceeds – otherwise an infinite loop is created that will relentlessly execute its statements.

The test expression is evaluated at the start of each iteration of the loop for a Boolean **true** value. When the evaluation returns **true** the iteration proceeds but when it returns **false** the loop is immediately terminated, without completing that iteration.

Note that if the test expression returns **false** when it is first evaluated the loop statements are never executed.

A **while** loop can be made to resemble the structure of a **for** loop, to evaluate a counter variable in its test expression, by creating a counter variable outside the loop and changing its value within the statements it executes on each iteration. For example, the outer **for** loop in the previous example can be recreated as a **while** loop like this:

```
int i = 1 ;

while ( i < 4 )
{
        System.out.println( "Outer Loop i=" +i ) ;
        i++ ;
}
```

This positions the counter initializer externally, before the while loop structure, and its updater within the statement block.

Beware

An infinite loop will lock the program as it continues to perform iterations – on Windows press **Ctrl + C** to halt.

1 Start a new program named "While" containing the standard main method
```
class While
{
        public static void main ( String[] args ) {          }
}
```

JAVA

While.java

2 Inside the main method, declare and initialize an integer variable named **num**
```
int num = 100 ;
```

3 Add a **while** loop to display the **num** variable's current value while it remains above zero
```
while ( num > 0 )
{
        System.out.println( "While Countdown: " + num ) ;
}
```

4 Insert an updater at the end of the **while** loop block to decrease the **num** variable's value by 10 on each iteration – thereby avoiding an infinite loop
```
num -= 10 ;
```

5 Save the program as **While.java** then compile and run the program to see the output

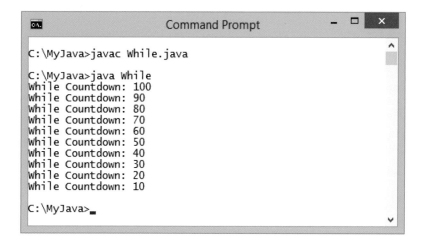

```
Command Prompt                              _  □  ×

C:\MyJava>javac While.java

C:\MyJava>java While
While Countdown: 100
While Countdown: 90
While Countdown: 80
While Countdown: 70
While Countdown: 60
While Countdown: 50
While Countdown: 40
While Countdown: 30
While Countdown: 20
While Countdown: 10

C:\MyJava>_
```

Don't forget

The assignment in this updater is shorthand for **num = (num - 10)**.

53

Doing do-while loops

A variation of the **while** loop structure, described on the previous page, employs the **do** keyword to create a loop with this syntax:

```
do
{
        statements-to-be-executed-on-each-iteration ;
}
while ( test-expression ) ;
```

Like the **for** loop and **while** loop, a **do while** loop repeatedly executes the statements it contains until a tested condition is met – then the loop ends and the program proceeds to its next task.

Unlike the **for** loop and **while** loop, the **do while** test expression appears after the block containing the statements to be executed. The test expression is evaluated at the end of each iteration of the loop for a Boolean **true** value. When the evaluation returns **true** the next iteration proceeds but when it returns **false** the loop is immediately terminated. This means that the statements in a **do while** loop are always executed at least once.

Note that if the test expression returns **false** when it is first evaluated the loop statements have already been executed once.

A **do while** loop can be made to resemble the structure of a **for** loop, to evaluate a counter variable in its test expression, by positioning the counter initializer outside the loop structure and its updater within the statement block – just as with a **while** loop.

All **for, while,** or **do while** loop structures containing just one statement to execute may, optionally, omit the curly brackets around the statement. But, if omitted, you will need to add curly brackets if additional statements are added to the loop later.

The choice of **for, while,** or **do while** loop is largely a matter of personal coding preference and purpose. A **for** loop structure conveniently locates the counter initializer, test expression, and updater in the parentheses after the **for** keyword. A **while** loop structure can be more concise – but you must remember to include an updater in the loop's statements to avoid an infinite loop. A **do while** loop simply adds the benefit of executing its statements once before evaluating its test expression – demonstrated by the **do while** loop described opposite.

Hot tip

Always enclose the statements to be executed by a loop within curly brackets – for clarity and improved code maintainability.

...cont'd

1 Start a new program named "DoWhile" containing the standard main method

```
class DoWhile
{
        public static void main ( String[] args ) {          }
}
```

DoWhile.java

2 Inside the main method, declare and initialize an integer variable named **num**

```
int num = 100 ;
```

3 Add a **do while** loop to display the **num** variable's current value while it is below zero

```
do
{
        System.out.println( "DoWhile Countup: " + num ) ;
}
while ( num < 0 )
```

4 Insert an updater at the end of the **do while** loop block to change the **num** variable's value on each iteration – thereby avoiding an infinite loop

```
num += 10 ;
```

5 Save the program as **DoWhile.java** then compile and run the program – see that the **num** variable never meets the test condition, but the statement executes once anyway

Don't forget

The assignment in this updater is shorthand for **num = (num + 10)**.

Breaking out of loops

The **break** keyword can be used to prematurely terminate a loop when a specified condition is met. The **break** statement is situated inside the loop statement block and is preceded by a test expression. When the test returns **true** the loop ends immediately and the program proceeds on to its next task. For example, in a nested loop it proceeds to the next iteration of its outer loop.

Break.java

1. Start a new program named "Break" containing the standard main method
```
class Break
{
        public static void main ( String[] args ) {            }
}
```

2. Inside the main method, create two nested **for** loops that display their counter values on each of three iterations
```
for ( int i = 1 ; i < 4 ; i++ )
{
        for ( int j = 1 ; j < 4 ; j++ )
        {
            System.out.println( "Running i="+i+" j="+j ) ;
        }
}
```

3. Save the program as **Break.java** then compile and run the program to see the output

```
                        Command Prompt              –  □  ×

C:\MyJava>javac Break.java

C:\MyJava>java Break
Running i=1 j=1
Running i=1 j=2
Running i=1 j=3
Running i=2 j=1
Running i=2 j=2
Running i=2 j=3
Running i=3 j=1
Running i=3 j=2
Running i=3 j=3
```

This program makes three iterations of the outer loop, which executes the inner loop on each iteration. A **break** statement can be added to stop the second execution of the inner loop.

4 Add this **break** statement to the beginning of the inner loop statement block, to break out of the inner loop – then recompile and re-run the program

```
if ( i == 2 && j == 1 )
{
        System.out.println( "Breaks innerLoop
                        when i=" +i+ " j=" +j ) ;

        break ;
}
```

Don't forget

Here, the **break** statement halts all three iterations of the inner loop when the outer loop tries to run it the second time.

```
Command Prompt                            - □ ×

C:\MyJava>javac Break.java

C:\MyJava>java Break
Running i=1 j=1
Running i=1 j=2
Running i=1 j=3
Breaks innerLoop when i=2 j=1
Running i=3 j=1
Running i=3 j=2
Running i=3 j=3
```

57

The **continue** keyword can be used to skip a single iteration of a loop when a specified condition is met. The **continue** statement is situated inside the loop statement block and is preceded by a test expression. When the test returns **true** that iteration ends.

5 Add this **continue** statement to the beginning of the inner loop statement block, to skip the first iteration of the inner loop – then recompile and re-run the program

```
if ( i == 1 && j == 1 )
{
        System.out.println( "Continues innerLoop
                        when i=" +i+ " j=" +j ) ;
        continue;
}
```

Don't forget

Here, the **continue** statement skips just the first iteration of the inner loop when the outer loop tries to run it for the first time.

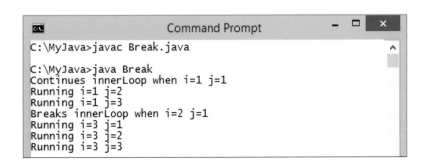

```
Command Prompt                            - □ ×

C:\MyJava>javac Break.java

C:\MyJava>java Break
Continues innerLoop when i=1 j=1
Running i=1 j=2
Running i=1 j=3
Breaks innerLoop when i=2 j=1
Running i=3 j=1
Running i=3 j=2
Running i=3 j=3
```

Returning control

The default behavior of the **break** and **continue** keywords can be changed to explicitly specify that control should return to a labeled outer loop by stating its label name.

Label.java

1 Start a new program named "Label" containing the standard main method
```
class Label
{
        public static void main ( String[] args ) {          }
}
```

2 Inside the main method, create two nested **for** loops that display their counter values on each of three iterations
```
for ( int i = 1 ; i < 4 ; i++ )
{
        for ( int j = 1 ; j < 4 ; j++ )
        {
            System.out.println( "Running i="+i+ " j="+j ) ;
        }
}
```

3 Save the program as **Label.java** then compile and run the program to see the output

```
 C:.                   Command Prompt              –  □   ×

C:\MyJava>javac Label.java

C:\MyJava>java Label
Running i=1 j=1
Running i=1 j=2
Running i=1 j=3
Running i=2 j=1
Running i=2 j=2
Running i=2 j=3
Running i=3 j=1
Running i=3 j=2
Running i=3 j=3

C:\MyJava>_
```

The syntax to label a loop requires a label name, followed by a : colon character, to precede the start of the loop structure.

4 Edit the start of the outer loop to label it "outerLoop"
```
outerLoop : for ( int i = 1 ; i < 4 ; i++ )
```

To explicitly specify that the program should proceed in the outer loop, state that loop's label name after the **continue** keyword.

⑤ Add this **continue** statement to the beginning of the inner loop statement block, to proceed at the next iteration of the outer loop – then recompile and re-run the program

```
if ( i == 1 && j == 1 )
{
        System.out.println( "Continues outerLoop
                        when i=" +i+ " j=" +j ) ;
        continue outerLoop ;
}
```

Here, the **continue** statement halts all three iterations of the inner loop's first run – by returning control to the outer loop.

```
Command Prompt                          _  □  ×

C:\MyJava>javac Label.java

C:\MyJava>java Label
Continues outerLoop when i=1 j=1
Running i=2 j=1
Running i=2 j=2
Running i=2 j=3
Running i=3 j=1
Running i=3 j=2
Running i=3 j=3
```

To explicitly specify that the program should exit from the outer loop, state that loop's label name after the **break** keyword.

⑥ Add this **break** statement to the beginning of the inner loop statement block, to exit the outer loop – then recompile and re-run the program

```
if ( i == 2 && j == 3 )
{
        System.out.println( "Breaks outerLoop
                        when i=" +i+ " j=" +j ) ;
        break outerLoop ;
}
```

Here, the **break** statement halts all further iterations of the entire loop structure – by exiting from the outer loop.

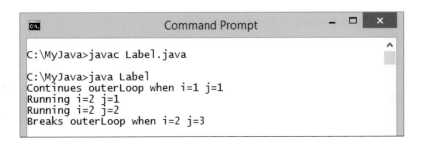

```
Command Prompt                          _  □  ×

C:\MyJava>javac Label.java

C:\MyJava>java Label
Continues outerLoop when i=1 j=1
Running i=2 j=1
Running i=2 j=2
Breaks outerLoop when i=2 j=3
```

Summary

- The **if** keyword performs a conditional test to evaluate an expression for a Boolean value of **true** or **false**

- An **if** statement block can contain one or more statements, which are only executed when the test expression returns **true**

- The **else** keyword specifies alternative statements to execute when the test performed by the **if** keyword returns **false**

- Combined **if else** statements enable a program to proceed by the process of conditional branching

- A **switch** statement can often provide an elegant solution to unwieldy **if else** statements by offering **case** options

- Each **case** option can be terminated by the **break** keyword so only statements associated with that option will be executed

- The **default** keyword can specify statements to be executed when all **case** options return **false**

- A loop repeatedly executes the statements it contains until a tested expression returns **false**

- The parentheses that follow the **for** keyword specify the loop's counter initializer, test expression, and counter updater

- Statements in a **while** loop and a **do while** loop must change a value used in their test expression to avoid an infinite loop

- The test expression is evaluated at the start of **for** loops and **while** loops – before the first iteration of the loop

- The test expression is evaluated at the end of **do while** loops – after the first iteration of the loop

- A loop iteration can be skipped using the **continue** keyword

- A loop can be terminated using the **break** keyword

- Nested inner loops can use labels with the **break** and **continue** keywords to reference the outer loop

4 Directing values

This chapter demonstrates how to direct data values using various Java programming constructs.

Casting type values

Handling values in Java programming requires correct data typing to be closely observed to avoid compiler errors. For example, sending a **float** type value to a method that requires an **int** type value will produce a compiler error. This means it is often necessary to convert a value to another data type before it can be processed.

Numeric values can be easily "cast" (converted) into another numeric data type using this syntax:

(*data-type* **)** *value*

Some loss of precision will occur when casting **float** floating point values into an **int** data type, as the number will be truncated at the decimal point. For example, casting a **float** value of 9.9 into an **int** variable produces an integer value of nine.

Interestingly, character values of the **char** data type can automatically be used as **int** values because they each have a unique integer representation. This is their numeric code value in the ASCII character set, which is supported by Java. The uppercase letter A, for instance, has the code value of 65.

Numeric values can be converted to the **String** data type using the **toString()** method of that value's data type class. This takes the numeric value as its argument, within the parentheses. For example, convert an **int num** variable to a **String** with **Integer.toString(num)**. Similarly, convert a **float num** variable to a **String** with **Float.toString(num)**. In practice, this technique is not always required because Java automatically converts concatenated variables to a **String** if any one of the variables has a **String** value.

More frequently, you will want to convert a **String** value to a numeric data type so the program can use that value arithmetically. A **String** value can be converted to an **int** value using the **Integer.parseInt()** method. This takes the **String** value as its argument, within the parentheses. For example, convert a **String msg** variable to an **int** with **Integer.parseInt(msg)**. Similarly, convert a **String msg** variable to a **float** with **Float.parseFloat(msg)**. When converting a **String** value to a numeric data type the **String** may only contain a valid numeric value, or the compiler will report an error.

All numeric classes have a **parse...** method and a **toString** method allowing conversion between **String** values and numeric data types.

1 Start a new program named "Convert" containing the standard main method

```
class Convert
{
        public static void main ( String[] args ) {        }
}
```

Convert.java

2 Inside the main method, declare and initialize a **float** variable and a **String** variable

```
float daysFloat = 365.25f ;
String weeksString = "52" ;
```

3 Cast the **float** value into an **int** variable

```
int daysInt = (int) daysFloat ;
```

4 Convert the **String** value into an **int** variable

```
int weeksInt = Integer.parseInt( weeksString ) ;
```

5 Perform arithmetic on the converted values and display the result

```
int week = ( daysInt / weeksInt ) ;
System.out.println( "Days per week: " + week ) ;
```

6 Save the program as **Convert.java** then compile and run the program to see the output

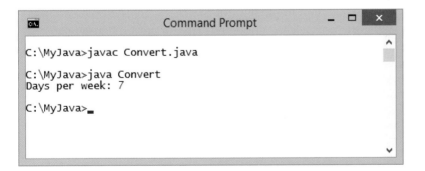

```
Command Prompt                              _  □  ×

C:\MyJava>javac Convert.java

C:\MyJava>java Convert
Days per week: 7

C:\MyJava>_
```

Creating variable arrays

An array is simply a variable that can contain multiple values – unlike a regular variable that can only contain a single value.

The declaration of an array first states its data type, using one of the data type keywords, followed by square brackets [ ] to denote that it will be an array variable. Next, the declaration states the array variable name, adhering to the normal naming conventions.

An array can be initialized in its declaration by assigning values of the appropriate data type as a comma-delimited list, enclosed within curly brackets. For example, the declaration of an integer array variable initialized with three values might look like this:

int[ ] numbersArray = { 1, 2, 3 } ;

The array is created of the length of the assigned list, allowing one "element" per value – in this case an array of three elements.

Stored values are indexed starting at zero and each value can be addressed by its element index position. The syntax to do so requires the array name to be followed by square brackets containing the element index. For instance, **numbersArray[0]** would address the first value stored in the example above (1).

Although the values stored in each element can be changed as simply as those of regular variables, the size of an array is determined by its declaration and cannot be changed later. Usefully, the total number of elements in an array is stored as an integer in the **length** property of that array. The syntax to address this figure just tacks a period and "length" onto the array name. For example, **numbersArray.length** would return the size of the array in the example above – in this case the integer 3.

Arrays can also be declared without assigning a list of initial values by using the **new** keyword to create an empty array "object" of a specified size. The number of required empty elements is stated in the assignment within square brackets after the appropriate data type. For example, the declaration of an empty integer array variable with three elements might look like this:

int[ ] numbersArray = new int[3] ;

The elements are assigned default values of zero for **int** and **float** data types, **null** for **String** data types, **\0** for **char** data types and **false** for **boolean** data types.

Beware

Remember that array indexing starts at zero. This means that **index[2]** addresses the third element in the array, not its second element.

1 Start a new program named "Array" containing the standard main method

```
class Array
{
        public static void main ( String[] args ) {          }
}
```

Array.java

2 Inside the main method, declare and initialize a **String** array with three elements

```
String[] str = { "Much ", "More", " Java" } ;
```

3 Declare an empty integer array with three elements

```
int[] num = new int[3] ;
```

4 Assign values to the first two integer array elements

```
num[0] = 100 ;
num[1] = 200 ;
```

5 Assign a new value to the second String array element

```
str[1] = "Better" ;
```

6 Output the length of each array and the content of all elements in each array

```
System.out.println( "String array length is " + str.length ) ;
System.out.println( "Integer array length is "+ num.length) ;
System.out.println( num[0] + "," +num[1]+ ","+num[2] ) ;
System.out.println( str[0] + str[1] + str[2] ) ;
```

7 Save the program as **Array.java** then compile and run the program to see the output

String values need to be enclosed within quotes.

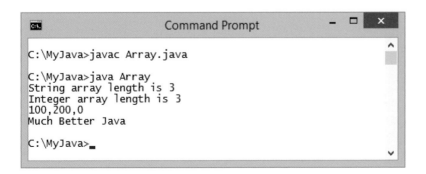

```
C:\MyJava>javac Array.java

C:\MyJava>java Array
String array length is 3
Integer array length is 3
100,200,0
Much Better Java

C:\MyJava>
```

Passing an argument

The standard Java code that declares the program's **main** method includes an argument within its parentheses that creates a **String** array, traditionally named "args":

public static void main(String[] args) { }

The purpose of the **args[]** array is to allow values to be passed to the program when it is called upon to run. At the command line a value to be passed to the program is added after a single space following the program name. For example, the command to pass the **String** "Java" to a program named "Run" would be **Run Java**.

A single value passed to a program is automatically placed into the first element of the **args[]** array, so it can be addressed by the program as **args[0]**.

It is important to recognize that the **args[]** array is of the **String** data type – so a numeric value passed to a program will be stored as a **String** representation of that number. This means that the program cannot use that value arithmetically until it has been converted to a numerical data type, such as an **int** value. For example, **Run 4** passes the number four to the program, which stores it as the **String** "4", not as the **int 4**. Consequently, output of **args[0]+3** produces the concatenated **String** "43", not the sum 7. The argument can be converted with the **Integer.parseInt()** method so that **Integer.parseInt(args[0])+3** does produce the sum 7.

A **String** containing spaces can be passed to a program as a single **String** value by enclosing the entire **String** within double quotes on the command line. For example, **Run "Java In Easy Steps"**.

Passing an argument to a program is most useful to determine how the program should run by indicating an execution option. The option is passed to the program as a **String** value in **args[0]** and can be evaluated using the **String.equals()** method. The syntax for this just tacks a period and "equals()" onto the array name, with a comparison **String** within the parentheses. For example, **args[0].equals("b")** evaluates the argument for the **String** value "b".

...cont'd

1 Start a new program named "Option" containing the standard main method

```
class Option
{
        public static void main ( String[] args ) {            }
}
```

Option.java

2 Inside the main method, write an **if** statement to seek an argument of "-en"

```
if ( args[0].equals( "-en" ) )
{
        System.out.println( "English option" ) ;
}
```

3 Add an **else** alternative onto the **if** statement to seek an argument of "-es"

```
else if ( args[0].equals( "-es" ) )
{
        System.out.println( "Spanish option" ) ;
}
```

4 Add another **else** alternative onto the **if** statement to provide a default response

```
else System.out.println( "Unrecognized option" ) ;
```

5 Save the program as **Option.java** then compile and run the program to see the output

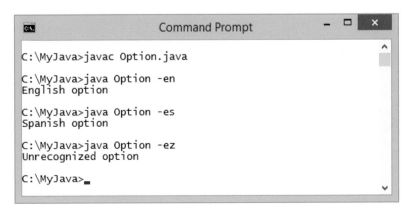

```
Command Prompt                                    _  □  ×

C:\MyJava>javac Option.java

C:\MyJava>java Option -en
English option

C:\MyJava>java Option -es
Spanish option

C:\MyJava>java Option -ez
Unrecognized option

C:\MyJava>_
```

Passing multiple arguments

Multiple arguments can be passed to a program at the command line, following the program name and a space. The arguments must be separated by at least one space and their values are placed, in order, into the elements of the **args[]** array. Each value can then be addressed by its index number as with any other array – **args[0]** for the first argument, **args[1]** for the second argument and so on.

The program can test the **length** property of the **args[]** array to ensure the user has entered the appropriate number of arguments. When the test fails the **return** keyword can be used to exit the **main** method, thereby exiting the program.

Args.java

Hot tip

The **return** keyword exits the current method. It can also return a value to the point where the method was called. See this in action in the example on page 99.

1 Start a new program named "Args" containing the standard main method
```
class Args
{
        public static void main ( String[] args ) {          }
}
```

2 Inside the main method, write an **if** statement to output advice and exit the program when there are not the required number of arguments – in this case three
```
if ( args.length != 3 )
{
    System.out.println( "Wrong number of arguments" ) ;
    return ;
}
```

3 Below the **if** statement, create two **int** variables – initialized with the values of the first argument and third argument respectively
```
int num1 = Integer.parseInt( args[0] ) ;
int num2 = Integer.parseInt( args[2] ) ;
```

4 Add a **String** variable, initialized with a concatenation of all three arguments
```
String msg = args[0] + args[1] + args[2] + "=" ;
```

...cont'd

5 Add this **if else** statement to perform arithmetic on the arguments and append the result to the **String** variable

```
if ( args[1].equals("+") )         msg += (num1 + num2);
else if ( args[1].equals("-") )    msg += (num1 - num2) ;
else if ( args[1].equals("x") )    msg += (num1 * num2) ;
else if ( args[1].equals("/") )    msg += (num1 / num2) ;
else msg = "Incorrect operator" ;
```

6 Insert this line at the end of the main method to display the appended **String**

```
System.out.println( msg ) ;
```

7 Save the program as **Args.java** then compile and run the program with three arguments – an integer, any arithmetical symbol + - x /, and another integer

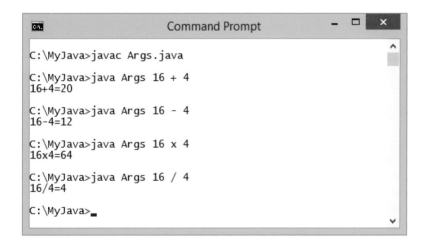

```
C:\MyJava>javac Args.java

C:\MyJava>java Args 16 + 4
16+4=20

C:\MyJava>java Args 16 - 4
16-4=12

C:\MyJava>java Args 16 x 4
16x4=64

C:\MyJava>java Args 16 / 4
16/4=4

C:\MyJava>
```

Hot tip

This program will report an error if non-numeric values are entered. See page 76 for details on how to catch errors.

8 Now, run the program with an incorrect second argument and with the wrong number of arguments

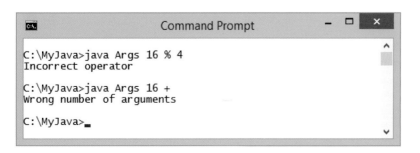

```
C:\MyJava>java Args 16 % 4
Incorrect operator

C:\MyJava>java Args 16 +
Wrong number of arguments

C:\MyJava>
```

Looping through elements

All types of loop can be used to easily read all the values stored inside the elements of an array. The loop counter should start with the index number of the first element then proceed on up to the final index number. The index number of the last element in an array will always be one less than the array length – because the index starts at zero.

It is useful to set the array **length** property as the loop's conditional test determining when the loop should end. This means that the loop will continue until the counter value exceeds the index number of the array's final element.

Loops.java

1 Start a new program named "Loops" containing the standard main method
```
class Loops
{
        public static void main ( String[] args ) {          }
}
```

2 Inside the main method, write an **if** statement to test whether any argument values have been entered into the **args[]** array from the command line
```
if ( args.length > 0 ) {   }
```

3 Insert a **for** loop inside the curly brackets of the **if** statement to output the value stored in each element
```
for ( int i = 0 ; i < args.length ; i++ )
{
        System.out.println( "args[" +i+ "] is | "+ args[i] ) ;
}
```

4 Save the program as **Loops.java** then compile the program and run it with the arguments **Java in easy steps**

```
 ▬                      Command Prompt            –  ▢  ✕

C:\MyJava>javac Loops.java

C:\MyJava>java Loops Java in easy steps
args[0] is | Java
args[1] is | in
args[2] is | easy
args[3] is | steps

C:\MyJava>_
```

5 Edit **Loops.java** to add a **String** array and a **while** loop to output the value stored in each element
```
String[] htm = { "HTML5", "in", "easy", "steps" } ;

int j = 0 ;
while ( j < htm.length )
{
        System.out.println( "htm[" +j+ "] is | " + htm[j] ) ;
        j++ ;
}
```

6 Save the changes then recompile and re-run the program

```
C:\MyJava>javac Loops.java

C:\MyJava>java Loops
htm[0] is | HTML5
htm[1] is | in
htm[2] is | easy
htm[3] is | steps
```

7 Edit **Loops.java** to add another **String** array and a **do while** loop to output the value stored in each element
```
String[] xml = { "XML", "in", "easy", "steps" } ;

int k = 0 ;
if ( xml.length > 0 ) do
{
        System.out.println( "\t\txml["+k+"] is | "+xml[k] ) ;
        k++ ;
} while ( k < xml.length ) ;
```

Hot tip

8 Save the changes then recompile and re-run the program

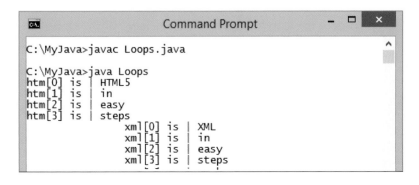

```
C:\MyJava>javac Loops.java

C:\MyJava>java Loops
htm[0] is | HTML5
htm[1] is | in
htm[2] is | easy
htm[3] is | steps
                xml[0] is | XML
                xml[1] is | in
                xml[2] is | easy
                xml[3] is | steps
```

Notice that the **do** statement is preceded by a conditional test to ensure the array is not empty before attempting to output the value of the first element.

Changing element values

The value stored in an array element can be changed by assigning a new value to that particular element using its index number. Additionally, any type of loop can be used to efficiently populate all the elements in an array from values stored in other arrays. This is especially useful to combine data from multiple arrays into a single array of totaled data.

Elements.java

1 Start a new program named "Elements" containing the standard main method

```
class Elements
{
        public static void main ( String[] args ) {          }
}
```

2 In the main method, add initialized **int** arrays representing monthly kiosk sales from all four quarters of a year

```
int[] kiosk_q1  = { 42000 , 48000 , 50000 } ;
int[] kiosk_q2  = { 52000 , 58000 , 60000 } ;
int[] kiosk_q3  = { 46000 , 49000 , 58000 } ;
int[] kiosk_q4  = { 50000 , 51000 , 61000 } ;
```

3 Add initialized **int** arrays representing monthly outlet sales from all four quarters of a year

```
int[] outlet_q1 = { 57000 , 63000 , 60000 } ;
int[] outlet_q2 = { 70000 , 67000 , 73000 } ;
int[] outlet_q3 = { 67000 , 65000 , 62000 } ;
int[] outlet_q4 = { 72000 , 69000 , 75000 } ;
```

4 Now, create an empty **int** array of 12 elements in which to combine all the monthly sales figures and an **int** variable in which to record their grand total value

```
int[] sum = new int[ 12 ] ;
int total = 0 ;
```

5 Add a **for** loop to populate each element of the empty array with combined values from the other arrays

```
for ( int i = 0 ; i < kiosk_q1.length ; i++ )
{
        sum[ i ]  = kiosk_q1[i] + outlet_q1[i] ;
        sum[i+3] = kiosk_q2[i] + outlet_q2[i] ;
        sum[i+6] = kiosk_q3[i] + outlet_q3[i] ;
        sum[i+9] = kiosk_q4[i] + outlet_q4[i] ;
}
```

6 Next, add a second **for** loop to output each of the combined monthly sales totals, and to calculate their grand total

```
for ( int i = 0 ; i < sum.length ; i++ )
{
        System.out.println( "Month "+ ( i+1 ) +
                                " sales:\t" + sum[i] ) ;
        total += sum[i] ;
}
```

7 Insert a final statement at the end of the main method to output the grand total

```
System.out.println( "TOTAL YEAR SALES\t" + total ) ;
```

8 Save the program as **Elements.java** then compile the program and run it to see the output

The counter number gets increased by one to produce the month numbers 1-12.

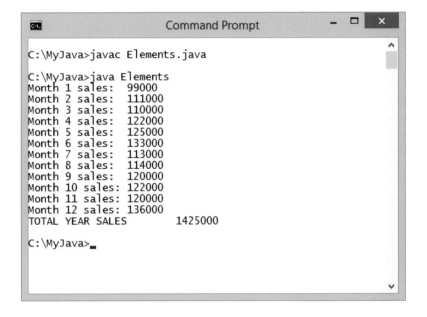

```
C:\MyJava>javac Elements.java

C:\MyJava>java Elements
Month 1 sales:   99000
Month 2 sales:   111000
Month 3 sales:   110000
Month 4 sales:   122000
Month 5 sales:   125000
Month 6 sales:   133000
Month 7 sales:   113000
Month 8 sales:   114000
Month 9 sales:   120000
Month 10 sales: 122000
Month 11 sales: 120000
Month 12 sales: 136000
TOTAL YEAR SALES         1425000

C:\MyJava>
```

Adding array dimensions

Arrays can be created to store multiple sets of element values, each having their own index dimension. Individual values are addressed in a multi-dimensional array using the appropriate index numbers of each dimension. For example, **num [1] [3]**.

A two-dimensional array might be used to record an integer value for each day of a business year, organized by week. This requires an array of 52 elements (one per week) that each have an array of seven elements (one per day). Its declaration looks like this:

int[][] dailyRecord = new int [52] [7] ;

This "array of arrays" provides an element for each business day. Values are assigned to a multi-dimensional array by stating the appropriate index numbers of each dimension. With the example above, for instance, a value can be assigned to the first day of the sixth week like this:

dailyRecord [5] [0] = 5000 ;

Each array has its own **length** property that can be accessed by specifying the dimension required. For the example above, the syntax **dailyRecord.length** returns a value 52 – the size of the first dimension. To access the size of the second dimension, the syntax **dailyRecord[0].length** returns the value of seven.

Two-dimensional arrays are often used to store grid coordinates, where one dimension represents the X axis and the other dimension represents the Y axis. For example, **point[3][5]**.

Three-dimensional arrays can be used to store XYZ coordinates in a similar way, but it can be difficult to visualize **point[4][8][2]**.

Nested loops are perfectly suited to multi-dimensional arrays as each loop level can address the elements of each array dimension.

Avoid using more than three dimensions in arrays – it will be confusing.

Dimensions.java

1 Start a new program named "Dimensions" containing the standard main method

```
class Dimensions
{
        public static void main ( String[] args ) {          }
}
```

2 In the main method, create a two-dimensional array to store XY coordinates
```
boolean[][] points = new boolean[5][20] ;
```

3 Define one Y point on each X axis
```
points[0][5] = true ;
points[1][6] = true ;
points[2][7] = true ;
points[3][8] = true ;
points[4][9] = true ;
```

Don't forget

Boolean variables are **false** by default.

4 Add a **for** loop to iterate through the first array index, adding a newline character at the end of each iteration
```
for ( int i = 0 ; i < points.length ; i++ )
{

        System.out.print( "\n" ) ;
}
```

5 Within the curly brackets of the **for** loop insert a second **for** loop to iterate through the second array index
```
for ( int j = 0 ; j < points[0].length ; j++ ) {     }
```

6 Within the curly brackets of the second **for** loop insert a statement to output a character for each element according to that element's Boolean value
```
char mark = ( points[i][j] ) ? 'X' : '-' ;
System.out.print( mark ) ;
```

7 Save the program as **Dimensions.java** then compile and run the program to see the output

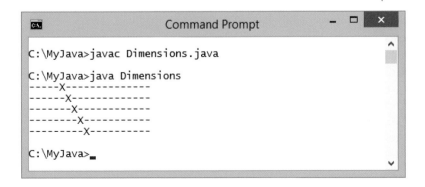

```
C:\MyJava>javac Dimensions.java

C:\MyJava>java Dimensions
-----X--------------
------X-------------
-------X------------
--------X-----------
---------X----------

C:\MyJava>
```

Catching exceptions

A program may encounter a runtime problem that causes an "exception" error, which halts its execution. Often this will be created by unexpected user input. A well-written program should, therefore, attempt to anticipate all possible ways the user might cause exceptions at runtime.

Code where exceptions might arise can be identified and enclosed within a **try catch** statement block. This allows the program to handle exceptions without halting execution and looks like this:

```
try
{
        statements where an exception may arise
}
catch( Exception e )
{
        statements responding to an exception
}
```

The parentheses following the **catch** keyword specify the class of exception to be caught and assign it to the letter "e". The top-level **Exception** class catches all exceptions. Responses can be provided for specific exceptions, however, using multiple **catch** statements to identify different lower-level exception classes.

The most common exceptions are the **NumberFormatException**, that arises when the program encounters a value that is not of the expected numeric type, and the **ArrayIndexOutOfBoundsException**, that arises when the program attempts to address an array element number that is outside the index size. It is helpful to create a separate response for each of these exceptions to readily notify the user about the nature of the problem.

Optionally, a **try catch** statement block can be extended with a **finally** statement block, containing code that will always be executed – irrespective of whether the program has encountered exceptions.

Hot tip

The **e.getMessage()** method returns further information about some captured exceptions.

...cont'd

1 Start a new program named "Exceptions" containing the standard main method

```
class Exceptions
{
        public static void main ( String[] args ) {          }
}
```

Exceptions.java

2 Inside the main method, write a **try** statement to output a single integer argument

```
try
{
        int num = Integer.parseInt( args[0] ) ;
        System.out.println( "You entered: "+ num ) ;
}
```

3 Add a **catch** statement to handle the exception that arises when the program is run without an argument

```
catch( ArrayIndexOutOfBoundsException e )
{ System.out.println( "Integer argument required." ) ;     }
```

4 Add a **catch** statement to handle the exception that arises when the program is run with a non-integer argument

```
catch( NumberFormatException e )
{ System.out.println( "Argument is wrong format." ) ;     }
```

5 Add a **finally** statement at the end of the program

```
finally { System.out.println( "Program ends." ) ;  }
```

6 Save the program as **Exceptions.java** then compile and run the program, trying to cause exceptions

```
Command Prompt                                    —  □   ×

C:\MyJava>javac Exceptions.java

C:\MyJava>java Exceptions
Integer argument required.
Program ends.

C:\MyJava>java Exceptions TWENTY
Argument is wrong format.
Program ends.

C:\MyJava>java Exceptions 20
You entered: 20
Program ends.
```

Summary

- Numeric values can be converted to other numeric data types by casting, and to the **String** type using the **toString()** method

- A **String** value can be converted to an **int** value using the **Integer.parseInt()** method and to a **float** using **Float.parseFloat()**

- An array is a variable that can contain multiple values, initialized as a list within curly brackets in its declaration

- An empty array object can be created using the **new** keyword

- The **length** property of an array stores an integer, which is the number of elements in that array

- Each element of an array can be addressed by its index number

- A program's **main** method creates a **String** array, traditionally named "args", to store command line arguments

- The first command line argument gets automatically stored in the **args[0]** element – as a **String** data type

- Multiple arguments being passed to a program from the command line must each be separated by a space

- Loops are an ideal way to read all the values stored within array elements

- Data from multiple arrays can be combined to form a new array of totaled data in each element

- Multi-dimensional arrays can store multiple sets of element values, each having their own index dimension

- A **try catch** statement block is used to anticipate and handle runtime exceptions that may arise

- The **Exception** class catches all exception errors, including **NumberFormatException** and **ArrayIndexOutOfBoundsException**

- A **try catch** statement can be extended with a **finally** statement block, containing code that will always be executed

5 Manipulating data

This chapter demonstrates how to manipulate program data using various Java library methods.

Exploring Java classes

Java has a vast library of pre-tested code arranged in "packages". Those providing functionality that is fundamental to the Java language itself are contained in the **java.lang** package, which is automatically accessible to the Java API (Application Programming Interface). This means that the properties and methods provided by the **java.lang** package are readily available when creating programs. For example, the standard output functionality provided by **System.out.println()** calls upon a method of the **System** class, which is part of the **java.lang** package.

Package contents are arranged in hierachical order allowing any item to be addressed using dot notation. For example, the **System** class contains an **out** property (field), which in turn contains a **println()** method – so can be addressed as **System.out.println()**.

The Java documentation provides information about every item available and can be used to explore the Java classes. It is available online at **http://docs.oracle.com/javase/8/docs/api** or can be downloaded for offline reference. The documentation is understandably large but familiarity with it is valuable. A good starting point is the API Overview page containing a list of every package together with a brief description.

 Start a web browser and open the API Overview page at **docs.oracle.com/javase/8/docs/api**

Don't forget

You can click on the Frames link to see a multi-pane view of the documentation.

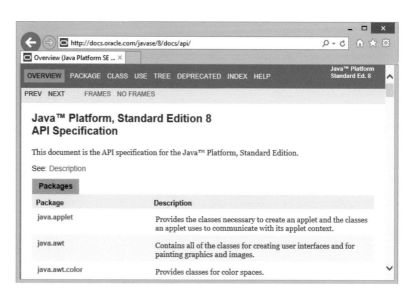

...cont'd

2   See the packages listed alphabetically on the Overview page as hyperlinks in the Packages table. Scroll down the page to find the **java.lang** package and click its hyperlink

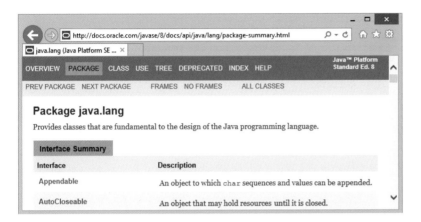

3   See the classes listed alphabetically in the Class Summary section of the Packages page as hyperlinks. Scroll down the page to find the **Math** class and click its hyperlink

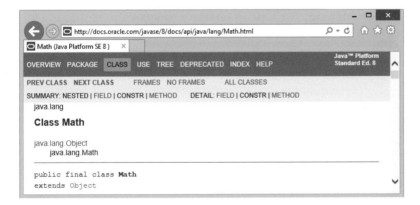

4   See all the special Math methods listed alphabetically in the Method Summary section of the Class page as hyperlinks. Click on any hyperlink to discover the purpose of that method and the syntax to use it

5   Click the Package item on the page menu to return to the **java.lang** package page and explore the other classes

Examine the information available via other items on the page menu to become more familiar with the documentation.

Doing mathematics

The **Math** class within the **java.lang** package provides two constant values that are often useful to perform mathematical calculations. **Math.PI** stores the value of Pi and **Math.E** stores the value that is the base of natural logarithms. Both these constant values are stored as **double** precision data types with fifteen decimal places.

Pi.java

1 Start a new program named "Pi" containing the standard main method
```
class Pi
{
          public static void main ( String[] args ) {          }
}
```

2 Inside the main method, declare and initialize a **float** variable from a command line argument and cast the **double Math.PI** constant into a second **float** variable
```
float radius = Float.parseFloat( args[0] ) ;
float shortPi = (float) Math.PI ;
```

3 Perform mathematical calculations using the cast value, assigning the results to more **float** variables
```
float circ = shortPi * ( radius + radius ) ;
float area = shortPi * ( radius * radius ) ;
```

4 Output the value of **Math.PI** and its cast **float** equivalent, followed by the results of the calculations
```
System.out.print( "With Pi commuted from " + Math.PI ) ;
System.out.println( " to " + shortPi + "..." ) ;
System.out.println( "A circle of radius " + radius + " cm" ) ;
System.out.print( "has a circumference of " + circ + " cm" ) ;
System.out.println( " and an area of " + area + " sq.cm" ) ;
```

Hot tip

The commuted value of Pi usually provides sufficient precision.

5 Save the program as **Pi.java** then compile and run the program to see the output

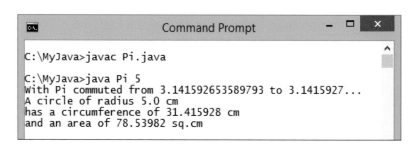

```
Command Prompt                              — □ ×

C:\MyJava>javac Pi.java

C:\MyJava>java Pi 5
With Pi commuted from 3.141592653589793 to 3.1415927...
A circle of radius 5.0 cm
has a circumference of 31.415928 cm
and an area of 78.53982 sq.cm
```

...cont'd

The **Math** class within the **java.lang** package provides many methods that are useful to perform mathematical calculations. Using **Math.pow()** a given number can be raised to a specified power. The parentheses require the number as its first argument and the power by which it is to be raised as its second argument. The **Math.sqrt()** method returns the square root of the number specified as its sole argument. Both methods return a **double** type.

1 Start a new program named "Power" containing the standard main method
```
class Power
{
        public static void main ( String[] args ) {          }
}
```

Power.java

2 Inside the main method, declare and initialize an **int** variable from a passed command line argument
```
int num = Integer.parseInt( args[0] ) ;
```

3 Perform mathematical calculations, casting the results into more **int** variables
```
int square = (int) Math.pow( num , 2 ) ;
int cube = (int) Math.pow( num , 3 ) ;
int sqrt = (int) Math.sqrt( num ) ;
```

4 Output the results of the calculations
```
System.out.println( num + " squared is " + square ) ;
System.out.println( num + " cubed is " + cube ) ;
System.out.println( "Square root of " + num + " is "+ sqrt ) ;
```

5 Save the program as **Power.java** then compile and run the program to see the output

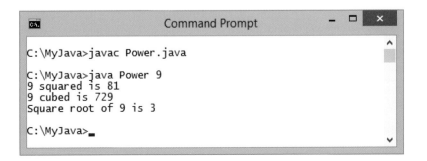

Don't forget

Both these examples could be improved by adding **try catch** statement blocks to anticipate user errors – see page 76 for details.

Rounding numbers

The **Math** class within the **java.lang** package provides three methods to round floating-point numbers to the nearest integer. Simplest of these is the **Math.round()** method that rounds a number stated as its argument up, or down, to the closest integer.

The **Math.floor()** method rounds down to the closest integer below and **Math.ceil()** rounds up to the closest integer above.

While the **Math.round()** method returns an **int** data type, both **Math.floor()** and **Math.ceil()** methods return a **double** data type.

Round.java

1 Start a new program named "Round" containing the standard main method
```
class Round
{
        public static void main ( String[] args ) {          }
}
```

2 Inside the main method, declare and initialize a **float** variable
```
float num = 7.25f ;
```

3 Output the rounded **float** value as an **int** value
```
System.out.println( num+"rounded is "+Math.round( num ) ) ;
```

4 Output the rounded **float** value as **double** values
```
System.out.println( num+" floored is " +Math.floor( num ) );
System.out.println( num+" ceiling is " + Math.ceil( num ) ) ;
```

5 Save the program as **Round.java** then compile and run the program to see the output

Hot tip

By default **Math.round()** will round up – so 7.5 would be rounded to 8.

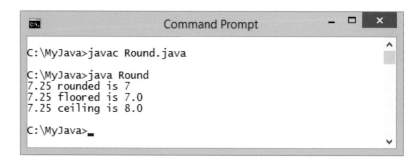

```
C:\MyJava>javac Round.java

C:\MyJava>java Round
7.25 rounded is 7
7.25 floored is 7.0
7.25 ceiling is 8.0

C:\MyJava>
```

...cont'd

The **Math** class within the **java.lang** package provides two methods to compare two numerical values. The **Math.max()** method and the **Math.min()** method each require two numbers to be stated as their arguments. **Math.max()** will return the greater number and **Math.min()** will return the smaller number.

The numbers to be compared can be of any numerical data type but the result will be returned as a **double** data type.

1. Start a new program named "Compare" containing the standard main method
```
class Compare
{
        public static void main ( String[] args ) {          }
}
```

Compare.java

2. Inside the main method, declare and initialize a **float** variable and an **int** variable
```
float num1 = 24.75f ;
int num2 = 25 ;
```

3. Output the greater value
```
System.out.println( "Most is " + Math.max( num1, num2 ) ) ;
```

4. Output the lesser value
```
System.out.println( "Least is " + Math.min( num1, num2 ) ) ;
```

5. Save the program as **Compare.java** then compile and run the program to see the output

Generating random numbers

The **Math** class within the **java.lang** package provides the ability to generate random numbers with its **Math.random()** method, which returns a **double** precision random number between 0.0 and 0.999. Multiplying the random number will specify a wider range. For example, multiplying by 10 will create a random number in the range of 0.0 to 9.999. Now, rounding the random number up with **Math.ceil()** will ensure it falls within the range of 1-10 inclusive.

Random.java

1. Start a new program named "Random" containing the standard main method
```
class Random
{
        public static void main ( String[] args ) {          }
}
```

2. Inside the main method, assign a random number to a **float** variable, and output its value
```
float random = (float) Math.random() ;
System.out.println( "Random number: " + random ) ;
```

3. Assign a multiplication of the random number to a second **float** variable, and output its value
```
float multiplied = random * 10 ;
System.out.println( "Multiplied number: " + multiplied ) ;
```

4. Assign a rounded integer of the multiplied random number to an **int** variable, and output its value
```
int randomInt = (int) Math.ceil( multiplied ) ;
System.out.println( "Random Integer: " + randomInt ) ;
```

5. Save the program as **Random.java** then compile and run the program to see the output

Hot tip

The Lottery program described opposite combines all three steps from this example into a single statement.

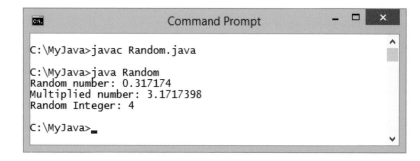

```
Command Prompt

C:\MyJava>javac Random.java

C:\MyJava>java Random
Random number: 0.317174
Multiplied number: 3.1717398
Random Integer: 4

C:\MyJava>
```

...cont'd

A sequence of six non-repeating random numbers within the
range 1-49 inclusive can be generated using **Math.random()** to
produce a random lottery selection.

1 Start a new program named "Lottery" containing the
standard main method

```
class Lottery
{
        public static void main ( String[] args ) {          }
}
```

Lottery.java

2 Inside the main method, create an **int** array of 50
elements, then fill elements 1-49 with integers 1-49

```
int[] nums = new int[50] ;
for( int i = 1 ; i < 50 ; i++ ) { nums[i] = i ; }
```

3 Shuffle the values in elements 1-49

```
for( int i = 1 ; i < 50 ; i++ )
{
        int r = (int) Math.ceil( Math.random() * 49 ) ;
        int temp = nums[i] ;
        nums[i] = nums[r] ;
        nums[r] = temp ;
}
```

4 Output only those values contained in elements 1-6

```
for ( int i = 1 ; i < 7 ; i++ )
{
        System.out.print( Integer.toString( nums[i]) + " " ) ;
}
```

5 Save the program as **Lottery.java** then compile it and run
the program three times to see three different sequences

87

Hot tip

This program is revisited
with a Graphical User
Interface in chapter 10.

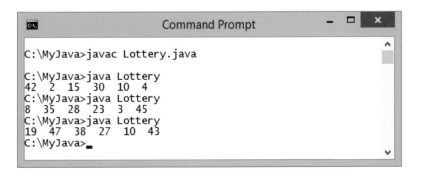

```
 C:\     ─    □    ×            Command Prompt

C:\MyJava>javac Lottery.java

C:\MyJava>java Lottery
42   2   15   30   10   4
C:\MyJava>java Lottery
8   35   28   23   3   45
C:\MyJava>java Lottery
19   47   38   27   10   43
C:\MyJava>_
```

Managing strings

In Java programming, a **String** is zero or more characters enclosed within quotation marks. So these are all valid **String** values:

String txt1 = "My First String" ;

String txt2 = "" ;

String txt3 = "2" ;

String txt4 = "null" ;

The empty quotes of **txt2** initialize the variable as an empty **String** value. The numeric value assigned to **txt3** is a **String** representation of the number. The Java **null** keyword, which normally represents the absence of any value, is simply a **String** literal when it is enclosed within quotes.

Essentially, a **String** is a collection of characters, each character containing its own data – just like elements in a defined array. It is, therefore, logical to regard a **String** as an array of characters and apply array characteristics when dealing with **String** values.

The **String** class is part of the fundamental **java.lang** package and provides a **length()** method that will return the size of a **String**, much like the **length** property of an array. Each **String** variable is created as an "instance" of the **String** class so its methods can be used by tacking their name onto the variable name using dot notation. For example, the syntax to return the size of a **String** variable named **txt** is **txt.length()**.

The **String** class within the **java.lang** package also provides an alternative to the **+** concatenation operator for joining **String** values together. Its **concat()** method requires a single argument specifying the second **String** to be appended. In use it is tacked onto the variable name of the first **String** using dot notation. For example, append **txt2** onto **txt1** using **txt1.concat(txt2)**.

Beware

Array.length is a property but **String. length()** is a method – so it must have trailing parentheses.

...cont'd

1 Start a new program named "StringLength" containing the standard main method

```
class StringLength
{
        public static void main ( String[] args ) {          }
}
```

StringLength.java

2 Inside the main method, create and initialize two **String** variables

```
String lang = "Java" ;
String series = " in easy steps" ;
```

3 Add another **String** variable and assign it the concatenated value of the other two **String** variables

```
String title = lang.concat( series ) ;
```

4 Output the concatenated **String** within quotation marks, together with its size

```
System.out.print( "\"" + title + "\" has " ) ;
System.out.println( title.length() + " characters" ) ;
```

5 Save the program as **StringLength.java** then compile and run the program to see the output

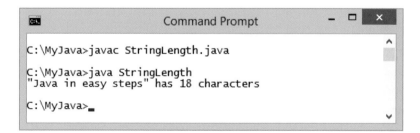

```
Command Prompt                                    — □ ✕

C:\MyJava>javac StringLength.java

C:\MyJava>java StringLength
"Java in easy steps" has 18 characters

C:\MyJava>_
```

Don't forget

Spaces are part of the **String** so are included in the character count – but the quotation marks are not included.

Comparing strings

The **String** class within the **java.lang** package provides the useful **equals()** method that was introduced on page 66 to evaluate a command line argument in the **args[0]** element. This can also be used to compare any two **String** values by tacking the method name onto the first **String** variable using dot notation, and specifying the **String** to be compared as its argument. For example, the syntax to compare **txt2** to **txt1** is **txt1.equals(txt2)**. When both **String** values have identical characters, in the same order, the method returns **true** – otherwise it returns **false**.

String values that use different letter case, such as "Java" and "JAVA", are not considered equal because the ASCII code values of the characters differ. For instance, the value of uppercase "A" is 65 whereas lowercase "a" is 97.

To compare an input **String** value, where the letter case entered by the user is uncertain, against a **String** value in the program it is often useful to transform the input into a particular case. For this purpose the **String** class provides a **toUpperCase()** method and a **toLowerCase()** method. The input **String** is specified as the argument and the method returns the transformed **String**.

A typical example might force a user-input password **String** to lowercase before comparing it to the correct password stored in all lowercase in a **String** variable within the program. This would allow the user to enter their password in uppercase, lowercase, or a mixture of both cases where case-insensitive passwords are permissible.

Dot notation allows methods to be tacked onto other methods so their operations can be performed in sequence. This means that **toLowerCase().equals()** can be used to transform a **String** value to lowercase and then compare that lowercase version against a specified argument.

Be sure to observe correct capitalization using a capital "C" in the toUpperCase and toLowerCase methods.

...cont'd

1 Start a new program named "StringComparison" containing the standard main method

```
class StringComparison
{
        public static void main ( String[] args ) {        }
}
```

StringComparison.java

2 Inside the main method, create and initialize a **String** variable with a correct lowercase password

```
String password = "bingo" ;
```

3 Add a **try catch** statement to catch the exception that occurs when no password argument is entered

```
try {    }
catch( Exception e )
{
        System.out.println( "Password required." ) ;
}
```

4 Insert this **if else** statement into the **try** statement block to evaluate the password argument entered by the user

```
if ( args[0].toLowerCase().equals( password ) )
{
        System.out.println( "Password accepted." ) ;
}
else
{
        System.out.println( "Incorrect password." ) ;
}
```

5 Save the program as **StringComparison.java** then compile and run the program with various arguments

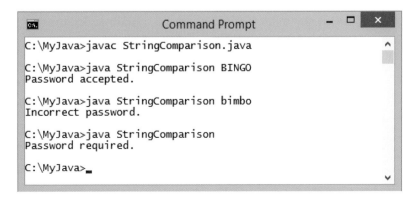

Command Prompt

```
C:\MyJava>javac StringComparison.java

C:\MyJava>java StringComparison BINGO
Password accepted.

C:\MyJava>java StringComparison bimbo
Incorrect password.

C:\MyJava>java StringComparison
Password required.

C:\MyJava>_
```

Searching strings

The **String** class within the **java.lang** package provides **startsWith()** and **endsWith()** methods to compare portions of a **String** value. These are especially useful to compare a number of **String** values and select those with common beginnings or common endings. When the **String** section matches the specified argument the method returns **true** – otherwise it returns **false**.

A portion of a **String** value can be copied by stating the position number of the first character to be copied as the argument to its **substring()** method. This will return a substring of the original **String** value, starting at the specified start position and ending at the end of the original **String**.

Optionally, the **substring()** method can take a second argument to specify the position number of the final character to be copied. This will return a substring of the original **String** value, starting at the specified start position and ending at the specified end position.

A **String** value can be searched to find a character or substring specified as the argument to its **indexOf()** method. Unusually, this method returns the numeric position of the first occurrence of the matched character or substring within the searched **String** value. Where no match is found the method returns the negative integer value of -1.

StringSearch.java

1 Start a new program named "StringSearch" containing the standard main method

```
class StringSearch
{
        public static void main ( String[] args ) {          }
}
```

2 Inside the main method, create an initialized **String** array of book titles

```
String[] books  =
{        "Java in easy steps", "XML in easy steps" ,
         "HTML in easy steps" , "CSS in easy steps" ,
         "Gone With the Wind" , "Drop the Defense" } ;
```

3 Create and initialize three **int** counter variables

```
int counter1 = 0 , counter2 = 0 , counter3 = 0 ;
```

4 Add a **for** loop to iterate through the **String** array, listing as output the first four characters of each title
```
for ( int i = 0 ; i < books.length ; i++ )
{
        System.out.print( books[i].substring( 0,4 ) + " | " ) ;
}
```

5 Insert a statement in the **for** loop block to count the titles found with a specified ending
```
if ( books[i].endsWith( "in easy steps" ) ) counter1++ ;
```

6 Insert a statement in the **for** loop block to count the titles found with a specified beginning
```
if ( books[i].startsWith( "Java" ) ) counter2++ ;
```

7 Insert a statement in the **for** loop block to count the titles found not containing a specified substring
```
if ( books[i].indexOf( "easy" ) == -1 ) counter3++ ;
```

8 At the end of the main method, add these statements to output the results of each search
```
System.out.println( "\nFound " + counter1 +
                                    " titles from this series" ) ;
System.out.println( "Found " + counter2 + " Java title" ) ;
System.out.println( "Found " + counter3 + " other titles" ) ;
```

9 Save the program as **StringSearch.java** then compile and run the program to see the output

The **!** NOT operator cannot be used to test if the **indexOf()** method has failed – because it returns an integer value, not a Boolean value.

Manipulating characters

The **String** class within the **java.lang** package provides the **trim()** method that is used to remove any whitespace from the beginning and end of the **String** specified as its argument. This method will remove all extreme spaces, newlines, and tabs, returning the trimmed version of that **String**.

An individual character in a **String** can be addressed by stating its index position within that **String** as the argument to its **charAt()** method. This method treats the **String** as an array of characters where the first character is at position zero – just like other arrays whose elements are indexed starting at zero. The first character in a **String** can be addressed as **charAt(0)**, the second character as **charAt(1)**, and so on.

As character indexing begins at zero, the final character in a **String** will always have an index number that is one less than the total number of characters in the **String**. This means that the final character in any **String** has the index number equivalent to **length() - 1**. The final character in a **String** named "str" can, therefore, be addressed as **str.charAt(str.length() -1)**.

All occurrences of a particular character in a **String** can be replaced by another character using its **replace()** method. This method requires two arguments that specify the character to be replaced and the character that is to take its place. For example, to replace all occurrences of the letter "a" with the letter "z" the syntax would be **replace('a' , 'z')**.

The **isEmpty()** method can be used to discover if a **String** contains no characters. This method will return **true** if the **String** is absolutely empty, otherwise it will return **false**.

CharacterSwap.java

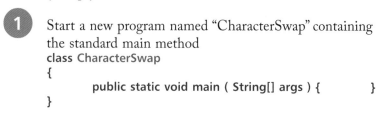

1 Start a new program named "CharacterSwap" containing the standard main method
```
class CharacterSwap
{
    public static void main ( String[] args ) {        }
}
```

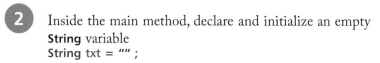

2 Inside the main method, declare and initialize an empty **String** variable
```
String txt = "" ;
```

3 Assign some characters to the **String** variable, if it is indeed empty, with both leading and trailing spaces
```
if ( txt.isEmpty() ) txt = "    Borrocudo    " ;
```

4 Output the **String** value and the number of characters it contains
```
System.out.println( "String:  " + txt ) ;
System.out.println( "Original String Length:  " + txt.length() ) ;
```

5 Remove the leading and trailing spaces, then output the **String** value and its size again
```
txt = txt.trim() ;
System.out.println( "String: " + txt ) ;
System.out.println( "String Length:  " + txt.length() ) ;
```

6 Output the first character in the **String**
```
char initial = txt.charAt(0) ;
System.out.println( "First Letter: " + initial ) ;
```

7 Now, output the last character in the **String**
```
initial = txt.charAt( ( txt.length() -1 ) );
System.out.println( "Last Letter: " + initial ) ;
```

8 Replace all occurrences of the letter "o" with letter "a"
```
txt = txt.replace( 'o' , 'a' ) ;
System.out.println( "String: " + txt ) ;
```

9 Save the program as **CharacterSwap.java** then compile and run the program to see the output

```
Command Prompt                                     _  □  ×

C:\MyJava>javac CharacterSwap.java

C:\MyJava>java CharacterSwap
String:         Borrocudo
String Length:  19
String: Borrocudo
String Length:  9
First Letter: B
Last Letter: o
String: Barracuda

C:\MyJava>_
```

Summary

- The Java documentation provides information about the methods and properties in each Java class

- Java classes that are fundamental to the Java language are contained in the **java.lang** package

- The **Math** class provides **Math.PI** and **Math.E** constants

- **Math.pow()** raises to a specified power and **Math.sqrt()** returns the square root of a specified number

- Numbers can be rounded to an integer value with **Math.round()**, **Math.floor()**, and **Math.ceil()**

- Numbers can be compared with **Math.max()** and **Math.min()**

- **Math.random()** returns a **double** precision random number between 0.0 and 0.999999999999999

- A **String** is zero or more characters enclosed in quote marks

- The **length()** method returns the size of its **String**, much like the **length** property of an array

- The **concat()** method of a **String** appends another **String** value

- The **equals()** method of a **String** only returns **true** when two **String** values have identical characters, in the same order

- Character case of a **String** can be changed using its **toUpperCase()** method and **toLowerCase()** method

- **String** values can be compared using the **startsWith()** and **endsWith()** methods of a **String**

- A substring can be sought in a **String** using its **indexOf()** and **substring()** methods

- The **isEmpty()** method only returns **true** when the **String** contains absolutely nothing

- Characters can be manipulated within a **String** value using its **trim()**, **charAt()**, and **replace()** methods

6 Creating classes

This chapter demonstrates how to create Java programs that employ multiple methods and classes.

Forming multiple methods

Programs are typically split into separate methods in order to create modules of code that each perform tasks, and that can be called repeatedly throughout the program as required. Splitting the program into multiple methods also makes it easier to track down bugs as each method can be tested individually. Further methods may be declared, inside the curly brackets that follow the class declaration, using the same keywords that are used to declare the main method. Each new method must be given a name, following the usual naming conventions, and may optionally specify arguments in the parentheses after its name.

Methods.java

1 Start a new program named "Methods" containing the standard main method

```
class Methods
{
        public static void main ( String[] args ) {          }
}
```

2 Between the curly brackets of the main method, insert statements to output a message and to call a second method named "sub"

```
System.out.println( "Message from the main method." ) ;
sub() ;
```

3 After the main method, before the final curly bracket of the class, add the second method to output a message

```
public static void sub()
{
    System.out.println( "Message from the sub method." ) ;
}
```

4 Save the program as **Methods.java** then compile and run the program to see the output

The syntax to call a method without arguments just needs the method name, followed by parentheses.

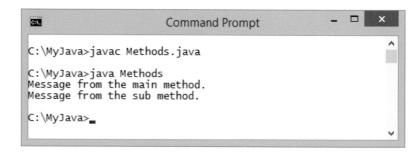

```
C:\MyJava>javac Methods.java

C:\MyJava>java Methods
Message from the main method.
Message from the sub method.

C:\MyJava>
```

98

...cont'd

A class may even contain multiple methods of the same name providing they each have different arguments – requiring a different number of arguments or arguments of different data types. This useful feature is known as method "overloading".

① Start a new program named "Overload" containing the standard main method

```
class Overload
{
        public static void main ( String[] args ) {          }
}
```

Overload.java

② Between the curly brackets of the main method, insert three statements calling different overloaded methods and passing them argument values

```
System.out.println( write( 12 ) ) ;
System.out.println( write( "Twelve" ) ) ;
System.out.println( write( 4 , 16 ) ) ;
```

③ After the main method, before the final curly bracket of the class, add the three overloaded methods to each return a **String** to the caller

```
public static String write( int num )
{         return ( "Integer passed is " + num ) ;    }

public static String write( String num )
{         return ( "String passed is " + num ) ;      }

public static String write( int num1 , int num2 )
{         return ( "Sum Total is " + ( num1 * num2 ) ) ;    }
```

④ Save the program as **Overload.java** then compile and run the program to see the output

```
Command Prompt                          _  □  ✕

C:\MyJava>javac Overload.java

C:\MyJava>java Overload
Integer passed is 12
String passed is Twelve
Sum Total is 64

C:\MyJava>_
```

Beware

The declaration for each of the overloaded methods must indicate that the method returns a **String** value, not **void**.

Understanding program scope

A variable that is declared inside a method is only accessible from inside that method – its "scope" of accessibility is only local to the method in which it is declared. This means that a variable of the same name can be declared in another method without conflict.

Scope.java

1 Start a new program named "Scope" containing the standard main method

```
class Scope
{
        public static void main ( String[] args ) {          }
}
```

2 Between the curly brackets of the main method declare and initialize a local **String** variable, then output its value

```
String txt = "This is a local variable in the main method" ;
System.out.println( txt ) ;
```

3 After the main method, before the final curly bracket of the class, add another method named "sub"

```
public static void sub( ) {          }
```

4 Between the curly brackets of the sub method declare and initialize a local **String** variable of the same name as the variable in the main method

```
String txt = "This is a local variable in the sub method" ;
System.out.println( txt ) ;
```

5 Insert a call to the sub method at the end of the main method

```
sub() ;
```

6 Save the program as **Scope.java** then compile and run the program to see the output

A counter variable declared in a **for** loop cannot be accessed outside the loop – its scope is limited to the **for** statement block.

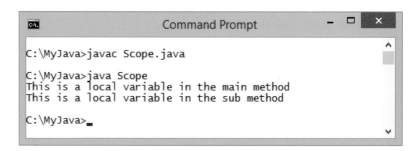

The **static** keyword that is used in method declarations ensures that the method is a "class method" – globally accessible from any other method in the class.

Similarly, a "class variable" can be declared with the **static** keyword to ensure it is globally accessible throughout the class. Its declaration should be made before the main method declaration, right after the curly bracket following the class declaration.

A program may have a global class variable and local method variable of the same name. The local method variable takes precedence unless the global class variable is explicitly addressed by the class name prefix using dot notation, or if a local variable of that name has not been declared.

7 Edit **Scope.java** by inserting a global class **String** variable constant of the same name as the local method variables
final static String txt =
         "This is a global variable of the Scope class" ;

8 Add a statement at the end of the main method to output the value of the global class variable
System.out.println(Scope.txt) ;

9 Comment out the line that declares the local variable in the sub method – so the output statement will now address the global variable of the same name
//String txt = "This is a local variable in the sub method" ;

10 Save the changes then recompile the program and run it once more to see the revised output

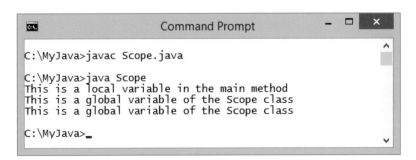

```
C:\MyJava>javac Scope.java

C:\MyJava>java Scope
This is a local variable in the main method
This is a global variable of the Scope class
This is a global variable of the Scope class

C:\MyJava>_
```

Hot tip

Use local method variables wherever possible to avoid conflicts – global class variables are typically only used for constants.

101

Forming multiple classes

In the same way that a program may have multiple methods larger programs may consist of several classes – where each class provides specific functionality. This modular format is generally preferable to writing the entire program in a single class as it makes debugging easier and provides better flexiblity.

The **public** keyword that appears in declarations is an "access modifier" that determines how visible an item will be to other classes. It can be used in the class declaration to explicitly ensure that class will be visible to any other class. If it is omitted, the default access control level allows access from other local classes. The **public** keyword must always be used with the program's main method, however, so that method will be visible to the compiler.

Multi.java

1. Start a new program named "Multi" containing the standard main method – including the **public** keyword as usual
```
class Multi
{
        public static void main ( String[] args ) {        }
}
```

2. Between the curly brackets of the main method declare and initialize a **String** variable, then output its contents
```
String msg = "This is a local variable in the Multi class" ;
System.out.println( msg ) ;
```

3. Output the contents of a class **String** variable constant named "txt" from a class named "Data"
```
System.out.println( Data.txt ) ;
```

Hot tip

The compiler will automatically find classes in adjacent external **.java** files – and create compiled **.class** files for each one.

4. Call a method named "greeting" from the Data class
```
Data.greeting() ;
```

5. Call a method named "line" from a class named "Draw"
```
Draw.line() ;
```

6. Save the program as **Multi.java**

7 Start a new file creating the Data class
```
class Data
{

}
```

Data.java

8 Declare and initialize a public class variable constant
```
public final static String txt =
        "This is a global variable in the Data class" ;
```

9 Add a public "greeting" class method
```
public static void greeting
{
        System.out.print( "This is a global method " ) ;
        System.out.println( "in the Data class" ) ;
}
```

10 Save the file as **Data.java** in the same directory as the **Multi.java** program

11 Start a new file creating a Draw class and a class "line" method for default access – without the **public** keyword
```
class Draw
{
  static void line()
  {
        System.out.println( "_____" ) ;
  }
}
```

Draw.java

12 Save the file as **Draw.java** in the same directory as the **Multi.java** program, then compile and run the program to see the output

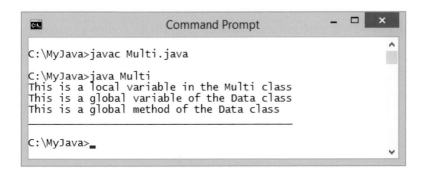

```
C:\MyJava>javac Multi.java

C:\MyJava>java Multi
This is a local variable in the Multi class
This is a global variable of the Data class
This is a global method of the Data class
_____

C:\MyJava>_
```

103

The **public** keword allows access from any other class but default access only allows access from classes in the same package.

Extending an existing class

A class can inherit the features of another class by using the **extends** keyword in the class declaration to specify the name of the class from which it should inherit. For example, the declaration **class Extra extends Base** inherits from the **Base** class.

The inheriting class is described as the "sub" class, and the class from which it inherits is described as the "super" class. In the example declaration above, the **Base** class is the super class and the **Extra** class is the sub class.

Methods and variables created in a super class can generally be treated as if they existed in the sub class providing they have not been declared with the **private** keyword, which denies access from outside the original class.

A method in a sub class will override a method of the same name that exists in its super class unless their arguments differ. The method in the super class may be explicitly addressed using its class name and dot notation. For example, **SuperClass.run()**.

It should be noted that a **try catch** statement in a method within a super class does not catch exceptions that occur in a sub class – the calling statement must be enclosed within its own **try catch** statement to catch those exceptions.

SuperClass.java

1 Start a new class named "SuperClass"
```
class SuperClass {          }
```

2 Between the curly brackets of the class add a method that outputs an identifying **String**
```
public static void hello( )
{
        System.out.println( "Hello from the Super Class" ) ;
}
```

3 Add a second method that attempts to output a passed argument, then save the file as **SuperClass.java**
```
public static void echo( String arg )
{
        try
        { System.out.println( "You entered: " + arg ) ;    }
        catch( Exception e )
        { System.out.println( "Argument required" ) ;    }
}
```

...cont'd

4 Start a new program named "SubClass" that extends the SuperClass class

```
class SubClass extends SuperClass
{
        public static void main ( String[] args ) {          }
}
```

SubClass.java

5 After the main method, add a method that outputs an identifying **String**, overriding the inherited method of the same name

```
public static void hello()
{
        System.out.println( "Hello from the Sub Class" ) ;
}
```

6 Between the curly brackets of the main method, insert a call to the overriding method and then explicitly call the method of the same name in the super class

```
hello() ;
SuperClass.hello() ;
```

7 Add a call to the other inherited method

```
echo( args[0] ) ;
```

8 Save the program as **SubClass.java** then compile and run the program without a command line argument

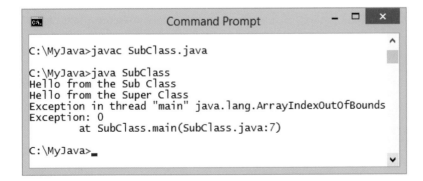

```
Command Prompt                                    –  □  ✕

C:\MyJava>javac SubClass.java

C:\MyJava>java SubClass
Hello from the Sub Class
Hello from the Super Class
Exception in thread "main" java.lang.ArrayIndexOutOfBounds
Exception: 0
        at SubClass.main(SubClass.java:7)

C:\MyJava>_
```

Don't forget

You can find more information for catching exceptions on page 76.

9 Edit **SubClass.java** to enclose the method call within its own **try catch** statement to catch exceptions, then recompile and re-run the program to see the problem resolved

Creating an object class

Real world objects are all around us and they each have attributes and behaviors that we can describe:

- Attributes describe the features that an object has

- Behaviors describe actions that an object can perform

For example, a car might be described with attributes of "red" and "coupe" along with an "accelerates" behavior.

These features could be represented in Java programming with a **Car** class containing variable properties of **color** and **bodyType** along with an **accelerate()** method.

Java is said to be an Object Oriented Programming (OOP) language because it makes extensive use of object attributes and behaviors to perform program tasks.

Objects are created in Java by defining a class as a template from which different copies, or "instances", can be made.

Each instance of the class can be customized by assigning attribute values and behaviors to describe that object.

The **Car** class is created as a class template in the steps described opposite – with the default attributes and behavior outlined above. An instance of the **Car** class is created in the steps described on page 109, inheriting the same default attributes and behavior.

1 Start a new template class named "Car"
```
class Car
{

}
```

FirstObject.java

2 Between the curly brackets of the **Car** class, declare and initialize two global **String** constants describing attributes
```
public final static String color = "Red" ;
public final static String bodyType = "Coupe" ;
```

3 Add a global method describing a behavior
```
public static String accelerate()
{
        String motion = "Accelerating..." ;
        return motion ;
}
```

4 After the **Car** class, start a new program class named "FirstObject" containing the standard main method
```
class FirstObject
{
        public static void main ( String[] args ) {        }
}
```

The **static** keyword declares class variables and class methods – in this case, as members of the **Car** class.

107

5 Between the curly brackets of the main method, insert statements to output the value of each **Car** attribute and call its behavior method
```
System.out.println( "Paint is " + Car.color ) ;
System.out.println( "Style is " + Car.bodyType ) ;
System.out.println( Car.accelerate() ) ;
```

6 Save the program as **FirstObject.java** then compile and run the program to see the output

Object classes are normally created before the program class containing the main method.

```
Command Prompt                                    – □ ×

C:\MyJava>javac FirstObject.java

C:\MyJava>java FirstObject
Paint is Red
Style is Coupe
Accelerating...

C:\MyJava>_
```

Producing an object instance

Each class has a built-in "constructor" method that can be used to create a new instance of that class. The constructor method has the same name as the class and is invoked with the **new** keyword.

Each instance of a class inherits the object's attributes and behaviors. The principle of inheritance is used throughout Java so that programs can use ready-made properties.

To be more flexible, object class templates can be defined in a file other than that containing the program. This means they can be readily used by multiple programs.

Car.java

1 Start a new file, repeating the **Car** class object template from the previous example

```
class Car
{
        public final static String color = "Red" ;
        public final static String bodyType = "Coupe" ;
        public static String accelerate()
        {
                String motion = "Accelerating..." ;
                return motion ;
        }
}
```

2 Save the file as **Car.java**

FirstInstance.java

3 Start a new program named "FirstInstance" containing the standard main method

```
class FirstInstance
{
        public static void main ( String[] args ) {          }
}
```

4 Between the curly brackets of the main method insert statements to output the value of each attribute of the **Car** class and call its behavior method

```
System.out.println( "Car paint is " + Car.color ) ;
System.out.println( "Car style is "+ Car.bodyType ) ;
System.out.println( Car.accelerate() ) ;
```

...cont'd

5 Now add a statement to create a **Porsche** instance of the **Car** class
```
Car Porsche = new Car() ;
```

6 Add statements to output the inherited value of each **Porsche** attribute and call its behavior method
```
System.out.println( "Porsche paint is " + Porsche.color ) ;
System.out.println( "Porsche style is " + Porsche.bodyType ) ;
System.out.println( Porsche.accelerate() ) ;
```

7 Save the program as **FirstInstance.java** alongside the **Car.java** template file then compile and run the program to see the output

You cannot address the **motion** variable directly – it is out of scope within the method declaration.

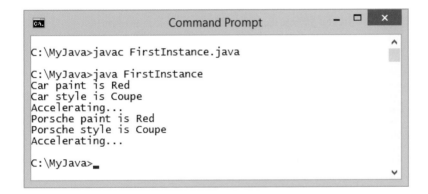

```
C:\MyJava>javac FirstInstance.java

C:\MyJava>java FirstInstance
Car paint is Red
Car style is Coupe
Accelerating...
Porsche paint is Red
Porsche style is Coupe
Accelerating...

C:\MyJava>
```

A virtual class is created for the new **Porsche** object that replicates the original **Car** class. Both these objects contain static "class variables" and a "class method" which are addressed using the class name and dot notation – as these members are globally accessible this is not considered good programming practice.

Whilst this example demonstrates how instances of an object inherit properties of the original class it is improved in the next example that uses non-static members to create "instance variables" and an "instance method" which cannot be addressed from outside that class – as these members are not globally accessible this is considered good programming practice.

The compiler automatically finds the **Car** class in the external **.java** file – and creates a compiled **.class** file for it.

Encapsulating properties

The **private** keyword can be used when declaring object variables and methods to protect them from manipulation by external program code. The object should then include **public** methods to retrieve the values and call the methods. This technique neatly encapsulates the variables and methods within the object structure. It is demonstrated in the following steps that reproduce the previous example – but with encapsulated attributes and method.

SafeInstance.java

1 Start a new class named "Car"
```
class Car
{

}
```

2 Between the curly brackets of the class, declare three private **String** variables to store object attributes
```
private String maker ;
private String color ;
private String bodyType ;
```

3 Add a private method describing a behavior
```
private String accelerate()
{
        String motion = "Accelerating..." ;
        return motion ;
}
```

4 Add a public method to assign passed argument values to each private variable
```
public void setCar( String brand , String paint , String style )
{
        maker = brand ;
        color = paint ;
        bodyType = style ;
}
```

5 Add another public method to retrieve the private variable values and to call the private method
```
public void getCar()
{
  System.out.println( maker + " paint is " + color ) ;
  System.out.println( maker + " style is " + bodyType ) ;
  System.out.println( maker + " is " + accelerate() + "\n" ) ;
}
```

6 After the end of the **Car** class, start another class named
"SafeInstance" containing the standard main method
```
class SafeInstance
{
        public static void main ( String[] args) {         }
}
```

7 Between the curly brackets of the main method, insert a
statement to create an instance of the **Car** class
```
Car Porsche = new Car() ;
```

8 Add a statement that calls upon a public method of the
Car class to assign values to its private variables
```
Porsche.setCar( "Porsche" , "Red" , "Coupe" ) ;
```

9 Now, add a statement to call upon the other public
method of the **Car** class to retrieve the stored atribute
values and call the private behavior method
```
Porsche.getCar() ;
```

10 Create another instance, assigning and retrieving values
```
Car Bentley = new Car() ;
Bentley.setCar( "Bentley" , "Green" , "Saloon" ) ;
Bentley.getCar() ;
```

11 Save the program as **SafeInstance.java** then compile and
run the program to see the output

An uninitialized **String**
variable has a **null** value
– so calling the **getCar()**
method before **setCar()**
will return a **null** from
each variable.

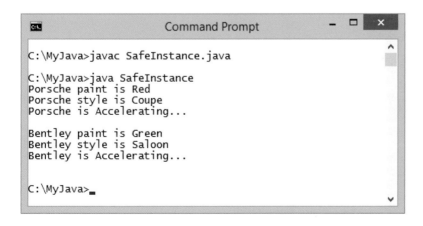

```
C:\MyJava>javac SafeInstance.java

C:\MyJava>java SafeInstance
Porsche paint is Red
Porsche style is Coupe
Porsche is Accelerating...

Bentley paint is Green
Bentley style is Saloon
Bentley is Accelerating...

C:\MyJava>
```

Constructing object values

An object's constructor method can be called directly in the object class to initialize object variables. This helps to keep the declarations and assignments separate and is considered to be good programming style. It is demonstrated in the following steps that reproduce the previous example with encapsulated attributes and method – together with initialization by the constructor:

Constructor.java

1 Start a new class named "Car"
```
class Car
{

}
```

2 Between the curly brackets of the class declare three private **String** variables to store object attributes
```
private String maker ;
private String color ;
private String bodyType ;
```

3 Add a constructor method that initializes all three variables with attribute values
```
public Car()
{
        maker = "Porsche" ;
        color = "Silver" ;
        bodyType = "Coupe" ;
}
```

Constructor method declarations do not state any return data type.

4 Add a private method describing a behavior
```
private String accelerate()
{
        String motion = "Accelerating..." ;
        return motion ;
}
```

5 Add a public method to assign passed argument values to each private variable
```
public void setCar( String brand , String paint , String style )
{
        maker = brand ;
        color = paint ;
        bodyType = style ;
}
```

6 Add another public method to retrieve the private variable values and to call the private method

```
public void getCar()
{
   System.out.println( maker + " paint is " + color ) ;
   System.out.println( maker + " style is " + bodyType ) ;
   System.out.println( maker + " is " + accelerate() + "\n" ) ;
}
```

7 After the end of the **Car** class, start another class named "Constructor" containing the standard main method

```
class Constructor
{
        public static void main ( String[] args ) {          }
}
```

8 Between the curly brackets of the main method, insert statements to create an instance of the **Car** class and retrieve the initial default values

```
Car Porsche = new Car() ;
Porsche.getCar() ;
```

9 Create another instance, assigning and retrieving values

```
Car Ferrari = new Car() ;
Ferrari.setCar( "Ferrari" , "Red" , "Sport" ) ;
Ferrari.getCar() ;
```

10 Save the program as **Constructor.java** then compile and run the program to see the output

```
Command Prompt                                    –  □  ×

C:\MyJava>javac Constructor.java

C:\MyJava>java Constructor
Porsche paint is Silver
Porsche style is Coupe
Porsche is Accelerating...

Ferrari paint is Red
Ferrari style is Sport
Ferrari is Accelerating...

C:\MyJava>_
```

Summary

- Splitting programs into multiple methods, which can be called upon when required, increases flexibility and makes it easier to track down bugs

- Overloaded methods have the same name but take different arguments

- Variables declared within a method have local scope but class variables have global scope throughout that class

- The **static** keyword is used to declare class methods and class variables – having global scope throughout that class

- The **public** keyword explicitly allows access from any class

- A class declaration can include the **extends** keyword to nominate a super class from which it will inherit

- The class name and dot notation can be used to explicitly address a particular class method or class variable

- Real world objects have attributes and behaviors that can be represented in programs by variables and methods

- Java objects are created as a template class from which instance copies can be made

- Each class has a constructor method that can be invoked using the **new** keyword to create an instance copy of that class

- Instances inherit the attributes and behaviors of the class from which they are derived

- Encapsulation protects instance variables and instance methods from manipulation by external classes

- The **private** keyword denies access from outside the class where the declaration is made

- An object's constructor method can be called to initialize variable attributes of that object

7 Importing functions

This chapter demonstrates how to import additional program functionality from specialized Java classes.

Handling files

Java contains a package named **java.io** that is designed to handle file input and output procedures. The package can be made available to a program by including an **import** statement at the very beginning of the .java file. This can use the * wildcard character to mean "all classes" in the statement **import java.io.* ; .**

The **java.io** package has a class named "File" that can be used to access files or complete directories. A **File** object must first be created using the **new** keyword and specifying the filename, or directory name, as the constructor's argument. For example, the syntax to create a **File** object named "info" to represent a local file named "info.dat" looks like this:

File info = new File("info.dat") ;

This file would be located in the same directory as the program but the argument could state the path to a file located elsewhere. Note that the creation of a **File** object does not actually create a file but merely the means to represent a file.

Once a **File** object has been created to represent a file its methods can be called to manipulate the file. The most useful **File** object methods are listed in this table, together with a brief description:

Method:	Returns:
exists()	true if the file exists – false if it does not
getName()	the filename as a String
length()	number of bytes in the file, as a long type
createNewFile()	true if able to create the new unique file
delete()	true if able to successfully delete the file
renameTo(File)	true if able to successfully rename the file
list()	an array of file or folder names as Strings

Don't forget

The filename specified as the constructor argument must be enclosed within quotes.

1 Start a new program that imports the functionality of all the **java.io** classes
import java.io.* ;

ListFiles.java

2 Add a class named "ListFiles" containing the standard main method

```
class ListFiles
{
        public static void main( String[] args ) {          }
}
```

3 Between the curly brackets of the main method, insert a statement to create a File object for a directory folder named "data"

File dir = new File("data") ;

4 Add an **if** statement to output the names of all files in that folder, or a message if the folder is empty

```
if ( dir.exists() )
{
        String[] files = dir.list() ;
        System.out.println( files.length + " files found..." ) ;
        for ( int i = 0 ; i < files.length ; i++ )
        {
                System.out.println( files[i] ) ;
        }
}
else
{       System.out.println( "Folder not found." ) ;          }
```

5 Save the program as **ListFiles.java** alongside a "data" folder containing some files, then compile and run the program to see the filenames listed as output

```
Command Prompt                          –  □  ×

C:\MyJava>javac ListFiles.java

C:\MyJava>java ListFiles
3 files found...
albums.ods
oscar.txt
xml.jpg

C:\MyJava>_
```

Reading console input

The **java.io** package allows a program to read input from the command line – interacting with the user. Just as the **System.out** field can send output to the command line, the **System.in** field can be used to read from it with an **InputStreamReader** object. This reads the input as bytes, which it converts into integer values that represent Unicode character values.

In order to read an entire line of input text the **readLine()** method of a **BufferedReader** object reads the characters decoded by the **InputStreamReader**. This method must be called from within a **try catch** statement to catch any **IOException** problems.

Typically, the **readLine()** method will assign the input to a **String** variable for manipulation by the program.

ReadString.java

1 Start a new program that imports the functionality of all the **java.io** classes
import java.io.* ;

2 Add a class named "ReadString" containing the standard main method
class ReadString
{
       public static void main(String[] args) {   **}**
}

3 Between the curly brackets of the main method, insert a statement to output a message prompting the user for input
System.out.print("Enter the title of this book: ") ;

4 Add a statement creating an **InputStreamReader** object, enabling input to be read from the command line
InputStreamReader isr =
        new InputStreamReader(System.in) ;

5 Create a **BufferedReader** object to read the decoded input
BufferedReader buffer = new BufferedReader(isr) ;

6 Declare and initialize an empty String variable in which to store the input
String input = "" ;

7 Add a **try catch** statement to read the input from the
command line and store it in the variable

```
try
{
        input = buffer.readLine() ;
        buffer.close() ;
}
catch ( IOException e )
{
        System.out.println( "An input error has occurred" ) ;
}
```

Hot tip

It is good practice to
call the **close()** method
of the **BufferedReader**
object when it is no
longer needed.

8 Output a message that includes the stored value
```
System.out.println( "\nThanks, you are reading " + input ) ;
```

9 Save the program as **ReadString.java** then compile and
run the program

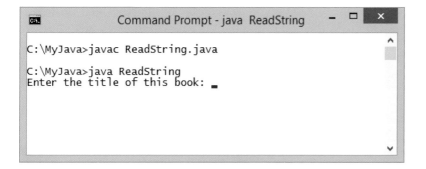

```
Command Prompt - java ReadString

C:\MyJava>javac ReadString.java

C:\MyJava>java ReadString
Enter the title of this book: _
```

10 Enter text as prompted then hit Return to see the output
message containing your input text

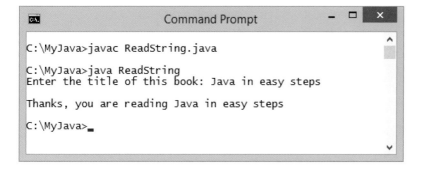

```
Command Prompt

C:\MyJava>javac ReadString.java

C:\MyJava>java ReadString
Enter the title of this book: Java in easy steps

Thanks, you are reading Java in easy steps

C:\MyJava>_
```

Reading files

The **java.io** package contains a class named **FileReader** that is especially designed to read text files. This class is a subclass of the **InputStreamReader** class that can be used to read console input by converting a byte stream into integers that represent Unicode character values.

A **FileReader** object is created using the **new** keyword and takes the name of the file to be read as its argument. Optionally, the argument can include the full path to a file outside the directory where the program is located.

In order to efficiently read the text file line-by-line, the **readLine()** method of a **BufferedReader** object can be employed to read the characters decoded by the **FileReader** object. This method must be called from within a **try catch** statement to catch any **IOException** problems that may arise.

Reading all lines in a text file containing multiple lines of text is accomplished by making repeated calls to the **readLine()** method in a loop. At the end of the file the call will return a **null** value, which can be used to terminate the loop.

1. Open a plain text editor, such as Windows Notepad, and write a few lines of text – for example, a famous verse from "The Ballad of Reading Gaol" by Oscar Wilde

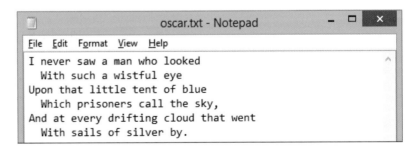

oscar.txt - Notepad

File Edit Format View Help

```
I never saw a man who looked
  With such a wistful eye
Upon that little tent of blue
  Which prisoners call the sky,
And at every drifting cloud that went
  With sails of silver by.
```

ReadFile.java

2. Save the text file as **oscar.txt** then start a new program that imports the functionality of all the **java.io** classes
import java.io.* ;

3. Add a class named "ReadFile" containing the standard main method
class ReadFile
{   public static void main(String[] args) {   }   }

4 Between the curly brackets of the main method, insert a
try catch statement
```
try {    }
catch ( IOException e )
{
        System.out.println( "A read error has occurred" ) ;
}
```

5 Between the curly brackets of the **try** block, insert a
statement to create a **FileReader** object
```
FileReader file = new FileReader( "oscar.txt" ) ;
```

The text file specified as
the **FileReader** argument
must be enclosed within
quotation marks.

6 Create a **BufferedReader** object to read the file
```
BufferedReader buffer = new BufferedReader( file ) ;
```

7 Declare and initialize an empty **String** variable in which
to store a line of text
```
String line = "" ;
```

8 Add a loop to read the text file contents into the variable
and output each line of text
```
while ( ( line = buffer.readLine() ) != null )
{        System.out.println( line ) ;        }
```

9 Remember to close the **BufferedReader** object when it is
no longer needed
```
buffer.close() ;
```

10 Save the program as **ReadFile.java**, alongside the text file,
then compile and run the program to see the output

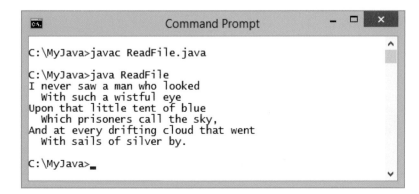

Writing files

In the **java.io** package the **FileReader** and **BufferedReader** classes, which are used to read text files, have counterparts named **FileWriter** and **BufferedWriter** that can be used to write text files.

A **FileWriter** object is created using the **new** keyword and takes the name of the file to be written as its argument. Optionally, the argument can include the full path to a file to be written in a directory outside that where the program is located.

The **BufferedWriter** object is created with the **new** keyword and takes the name of the **FileWriter** object as its argument. Text can then be written with the **write()** method of the **BufferedWriter** object and lines separated by calling its **newLine()** method. These methods should be called from within a **try catch** statement to catch any **IOException** problems that may arise.

If a file of the specified name already exists, its contents will be overwritten by the **write()** method, otherwise a new file of that name will be created and its contents written.

WriteFile.java

1 Start a new program that imports the functionality of all the **java.io** classes
import java.io.* ;

2 Add a class named "WriteFile" containing the standard main method
class WriteFile
{
       public static void main (String[] args) {   **}**
}

3 Between the curly brackets of the main method, insert a **try catch** statement
try {   **}**
catch (IOException e)
{
      System.out.println("A write error has occurred") ;
}

4 Between the curly brackets of the **try** block, insert a statement to create a **FileWriter** object for a text file named "tam.txt"
FileWriter file = new FileWriter("tam.txt") ;

...cont'd

5 Create a **BufferedWriter** object to write the file
```
BufferedWriter buffer = new BufferedWriter( file ) ;
```

6 Add statements to write lines of text and newline
characters into the text file – for example, a translated
verse from "Tam O'Shanter" by Robert Burns
```
buffer.write( "The wind blew as if it had blown its last" ) ;
        buffer.newLine() ;
buffer.write( "The rattling showers rose on its blast" ) ;
        buffer.newLine() ;
buffer.write( "The speedy gleams the darkness swallowed" ) ;
        buffer.newLine() ;
buffer.write( "Loud, deep and long the thunder bellowed" ) ;
        buffer.newLine() ;
buffer.write( "That night a child might understand" ) ;
        buffer.newLine() ;
buffer.write( "The devil had business on his hand." ) ;
```

7 Remember to close the **BufferedWriter** object when it is
no longer needed
```
buffer.close() ;
```

8 Save the program as **WriteFile.java** then compile and run
the program to write the text file alongside the program

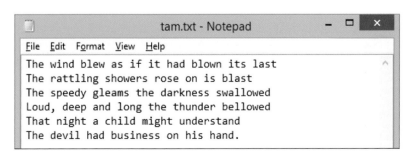

You can call the
append() method of the
BufferedWriter object to
add text – rather than
overwriting text with the
write() method.

Sorting array elements

Java contains a package named **java.util** that provides useful utilities for handling collections of data. The package can be made available to a program by including an **import** statement at the very beginning of the **.java** file. This can use the * wildcard character to mean "all classes" in the statement **import java.util.*** ; .

The **java.util** package has a class named "Arrays" that has methods which can be used to manipulate arrays. Its functionality can be made available to the program by importing all classes from the **java.util** package or, where the program only requires a single class, the **import** statement can import just that specific class. For example, the program can import the **Arrays** class with the statement **import java.util.Arrays** ; .

The **Arrays** class has a **sort()** method that can rearrange the contents of array elements alphabetically and numerically.

Sort.java

1 Start a new program that imports the functionality of all methods in the **java.util.Arrays** class
```
import java.util.Arrays ;
```

2 Add a class named "Sort" containing the standard main method
```
class Sort
{        public static void main( String[] args ) { }        }
```

Hot tip

See page 99 for more on overloading methods.

3 After the main method, insert a method to display all element contents of a passed **String** array
```
public static void display( String[] elems )
{
        System.out.println( "\nString Array:" ) ;
        for ( int i = 0 ; i < elems.length ; i++ )
        System.out.println( "Element "+i+" is "+elems[i] ) ;
}
```

4 Add an overloaded version of the **display()** method to display all element contents of a passed **int** array
```
public static void display( int[] elems )
{
        System.out.println( "\nInteger Array:" ) ;
        for ( int i = 0 ; i < elems.length ; i++ )
        System.out.println( "Element "+i+" is "+elems[i] ) ;
}
```

...cont'd

5 Between the curly brackets of the main method, declare and initialize a **String** array and an **int** array
String[] names = { "Mike" , "Dave" , "Andy" } ;
int[] nums = { 200 , 300 , 100 } ;

6 Output the contents of all elements in each array
display(names) ;
display(nums) ;

7 Sort the element contents of both arrays
Arrays.sort(names) ;
Arrays.sort(nums) ;

8 Output the contents of all elements in each array again
display(names) ;
display(nums) ;

9 Save the program as **Sort.java** then compile and run the program to see the output

The **for** loops in this example each execute a single statement so no curly brackets are required – but they could be added for clarity.

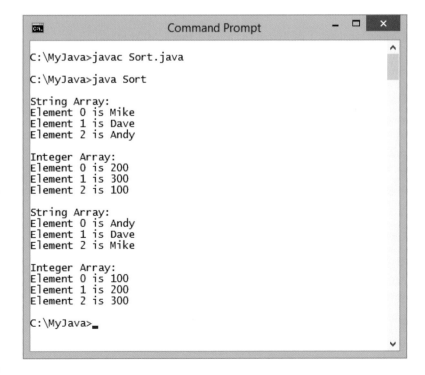

```
C:\MyJava>javac Sort.java

C:\MyJava>java Sort

String Array:
Element 0 is Mike
Element 1 is Dave
Element 2 is Andy

Integer Array:
Element 0 is 200
Element 1 is 300
Element 2 is 100

String Array:
Element 0 is Andy
Element 1 is Dave
Element 2 is Mike

Integer Array:
Element 0 is 100
Element 1 is 200
Element 2 is 300

C:\MyJava>_
```

Making array lists

The **java.util** package contains a class named **ArrayList** that stores data in an ordered "Collection" (resizable sequence) of list elements. This can be made available to a program by importing the specific class with **import java.util.ArrayList;**. A list may contain duplicate elements and an **ArrayList** object has useful methods that allow manipulation of stored values by specifying their element index number. For example, the list's method call **get(0)** will retrieve the value stored in the first element whereas **remove(1)** will remove the second list element.

Element values can be modified by specifying the index number and new value as arguments to the list's **set()** method. Elements can be added to the list at a particular position by specifying the index number and value as arguments to the list's **add()** method. The list expands to accommodate additional elements by moving the element values along the index.

An **ArrayList** object is simply created using the **new** keyword but, like other Java collections, the statement must specify which generic type of item the list may contain. Typically, a list may contain String items so **ArrayList** must have a **<String>** suffix.

Collections, such as **ArrayList**, have a **forEach()** method that iterates over each element in the list. This makes it easy to loop through all items contained in the list.

Each stored list item can be conveniently referenced in turn by specifying a "lambda expression" as the argument to the **forEach()** method. Lambda expressions are simply short anonymous (un-named) methods that can be specified in the location they are to be executed. They begin with parentheses, to contain any arguments, then have a **->** character sequence followed by the statement block, with this syntax:

(argument/s) -> { statement/s }

The data type of the arguments can be explicitly declared or it can be inferred from the context – **(String x)** can be simply **(x)**. Additionally, the curly brackets can be omitted if the lambda expression statement block contains only one statement.

With a list's **forEach()** method the value of the current element in the iteration can be passed to the lambda expression as its argument, then displayed in output by its statement.

Hot tip

You can discover how many elements a list currently has by calling its **size()** method.

Lambda expressions were introduced in Java 8 to enable succinct anonymous methods.

1 Start a new program that imports the functionality of all methods in the **java.util.ArrayList** class

```
import java.util.ArrayList ;
```

Lists.java

2 Add a class named "Lists" containing the standard main method

```
class Lists
{          public static void main( String[] args ) { }          }
```

3 Between the curly brackets of the main method, insert a statement to create a String **ArrayList** object named "list"

```
ArrayList<String> list = new ArrayList<String>() ;
```

4 Next, add statements to populate the list elements with String values then display the entire list

```
list.add( "Alpha" ) ;
list.add( "Delta" ) ;
list.add( "Charlie" ) ;
System.out.println( "List: " + list ) ;
```

As with regular arrays elements in an ArrayList have a zero-based index.

5 Now, identify the current value in the second element then replace it with a new String

```
System.out.println( "Replacing: " + list.get(1) + "\n" ) ;
list.set( 1, "Bravo" ) ;
```

6 Finally, iterate through the list and display the String value now stored in each element

```
list.forEach( ( x ) -> System.out.println( "Item: " + x ) ) ;
```

7 Save the program as **Lists.java** then compile and run the program to see the output

The graphical Java Swing **JComboBox** component that is introduced on page 142 holds a dropdown list of options, so must also specify its generic data type when that object gets created.

```
C:\MyJava>javac Lists.java

C:\MyJava>java Lists
List: [Alpha, Delta, Charlie]
Replacing: Delta

Item: Alpha
Item: Bravo
Item: Charlie

C:\MyJava>
```

Managing dates

The **java.time** package contains a class named **LocalDateTime** that has useful methods to extract specific fields from a **LocalDateTime** object that describe a particular point in time. These can be made available to a program by importing the specific class with **import java.time.LocalDateTime;** or by importing all classes in this package using the wildcard with **import java.time.*** ; .

A new **LocalDateTime** object can be created with fields describing the current date and time using its **now()** method. The fields are initialized from the system clock for the current locale.

The value within an individual field can be retrieved using an appropriate method of the **LocalDateTime** object. For example, the value of the year field can be retrieved using its **getYear()** method. Similarly, any field can be changed using an appropriate method of the **LocalDateTime** object to specify a replacement value. For example, the value of the year field can be changed by specifying a new year value as an argument to its **withYear()** method.

The **java.time** package was introduced in Java 8 to make it easier to work with dates and times.

DateTime.java

1 Start a new program that imports the functionality of all methods in the **java.time.LocalDateTime** class
import java.time.LocalDateTime ;

2 Add a class named "DateTime" containing the standard main method
```
class DateTime
{
        public static void main ( String [] args ) {          }
}
```

3 Between the curly brackets of the main method, insert a statement to create a current **LocalDateTime** object
LocalDateTime date = LocalDateTime.now() ;

4 Output the current date and time details
System.out.println("\nIt is now " + date) ;

5 Increment the year and output the revised date and time
date = date.withYear(2018) ;
System.out.println("\nDate is now " + date) ;

6 Output individual **LocalDateTime** fields of the revised date

```
String fields = "\nYear:\t\t\t" + date.getYear() ;

fields += "\nMonth:\t\t\t" + date.getMonth() ;

fields += "\nMonth Number:\t\t" + date.getMonthValue() ;

fields += "\nDay:\t\t\t" + date.getDayOfWeek() ;

fields += "\nDay Number:\t\t" + date.getDayOfMonth() ;

fields += "\nDay Number Of Year:\t" + date.getDayOfYear() ;

fields += "\nHour (0-23):\t\t" + date.getHour() ;

fields += "\nMinute:\t\t\t" + date.getMinute() ;

fields += "\nSecond:\t\t\t"  + date.getSecond() ;

System.out.println( fields ) ;
```

Concatenating a **String** like this means the program makes just one call to **println()** to output field details – this is more efficient than calling **println()** many times to output each individual field separately.

7 Save the program as **DateTime.java** then compile and run the program to see the output

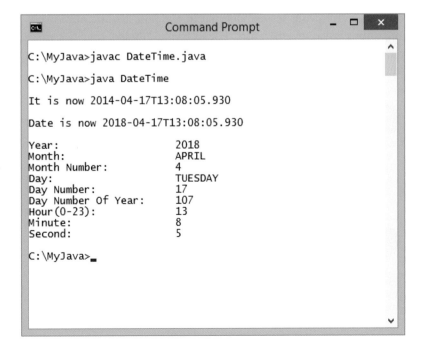

```
C:\MyJava>javac DateTime.java

C:\MyJava>java DateTime

It is now 2014-04-17T13:08:05.930

Date is now 2018-04-17T13:08:05.930

Year:                   2018
Month:                  APRIL
Month Number:           4
Day:                    TUESDAY
Day Number:             17
Day Number Of Year:     107
Hour(0-23):             13
Minute:                 8
Second:                 5

C:\MyJava>
```

Alternatively, you can use the **ZonedDateTime** class instead of **LocalDateTime** if you also require a time zone field.

The **java.time.format** package was introduced in Java 8 to make it easier to specify date format patterns.

Formatting numbers

Java contains a package named **java.text** that provides useful classes for formatting numbers and currency. The package can be made available to a program by including an **import** statement at the very beginning of the **.java** file. This can use the * wildcard character to mean "all classes" in the statement **import java.text.*** ;. Alternatively, specific classes can be imported by name.

The **java.text** package has a class named "NumberFormat" that has methods which can be used to format numerical values for output – adding group separators, currency signs, and percentage signs.

The method used to create a new **NumberFormat** object determines its formatting type – **getNumberInstance()** for group separators, **getCurrencyInstance()** for currency signs, and **getPercentInstance()** for percentage signs. Formatting is applied by specifying the numerical value to be formatted as the argument to the **format()** method of the **NumberFormat** object.

The **java.time.format** package has a **DateTimeFormatter** class that can be used to format **java.time** dates and time objects. A **DateTimeFormatter** object contains a formatter pattern that is specified as a string argument to its **ofPattern()** method. The formatter comprises letters, defined in the Java documentation, and your choice of separators. For example, **"M/d/y"** specifies the month, day, and year, separated by slashes. The format is applied by specifying the formatter as the argument to the **format()** method of a **java.time** date and time object.

Formats.java

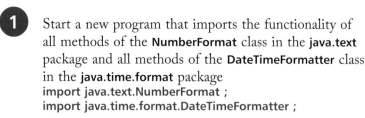

① Start a new program that imports the functionality of all methods of the **NumberFormat** class in the **java.text** package and all methods of the **DateTimeFormatter** class in the **java.time.format** package

```
import java.text.NumberFormat ;
import java.time.format.DateTimeFormatter ;
```

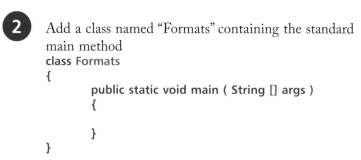

② Add a class named "Formats" containing the standard main method

```
class Formats
{
        public static void main ( String [] args )
        {

        }
}
```

3 Between the curly brackets of the main method, insert
statements to output a number with group separators
```
NumberFormat nf = NumberFormat.getNumberInstance() ;
System.out.println( "\nNumber: " + nf.format(123456789) ) ;
```

4 Add statements to output a number with a currency sign
```
NumberFormat cf = NumberFormat.getCurrencyInstance() ;
System.out.println( "\nCurrency: " + cf.format(1234.50f) ) ;
```

Hot tip

5 Add statements to output a number with a percent sign
```
NumberFormat pf = NumberFormat.getPercentInstance() ;
System.out.println( "\nPercent: " + pf.format( 0.75f ) ) ;
```

A statement can address
a class that has not
been imported by using
its full package address
– as seen here in the
statement creating a
LocalDateTime object.

6 Add a statement creating a current **LocalDateTime** object
```
java.time.LocalDateTime now =
        java.time.LocalDateTime.now() ;
```

7 Add statements to output a formatted numerical date
```
DateTimeFormatter df =
        DateTimeFormatter.ofPattern( "MMM d, yyy" ) ;
System.out.println( "\nDate: " + now.format( df ) ) ;
```

8 Add statements to output a formatted numerical time
```
DateTimeFormatter tf =
        DateTimeFormatter.ofPattern( "h:m a" ) ;
System.out.println( "\nTime: " + now.format( tf ) ) ;
```

9 Save the program as **Formats.java** then compile and run
the program to see the formatted output

Beware

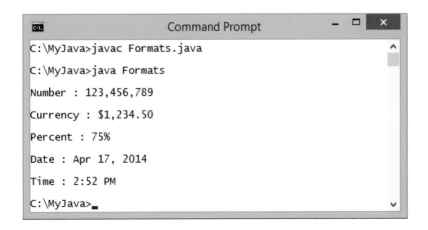

Pattern letters are case
sensitive – refer to
the documentation to
discover the full details
of possible patterns.

Summary

- One or more **import** statements can be included at the start of a program to make the functionality of other classes available

- An **import** statement can import all classes in a package with a * wildcard character, or individual classes by name

- The **java.io** package has classes that are designed to handle input and output procedures

- A **File** object can be used to access files and directories

- The **InputStreamReader** object decodes input bytes into characters and the **BufferedReader** reads its decoded characters

- A **FileReader** object can be used to decode text file bytes into characters for reading by a **BufferedReader** object

- A **FileWriter** object and **BufferedWriter** object can create and update text files

- The **java.util** package contains utilities for handling collections of data, such as array manipulation with its **Arrays** class

- The **java.util** package also contains an **ArrayList** class that has methods to easily manipulate sequenced list items

- An **ArrayList** object is a Collection that must specify the generic type of item that list may contain, such as **<String>**

- A lambda expression is an anonymous method that can be specified where it is to be executed

- The **java.time** package contains a **LocalDateTime** class that provides fields for date and time components

- The **java.text** package contains a **NumberFormat** class that can format numbers and currency

- The **java.time.format** package contains a **DateTimeFormatter** class that can specify patterns to format dates and times

8 Building interfaces

This chapter demonstrates how to use Java Swing components to create a graphical program interface.

Creating a window

Programs can provide a graphical user interface (GUI) using the "Swing" components of the Java library. The **javax.swing** package contains classes to create a variety of components using the style of the native operating system. These can be made available to a program by including the initial statement **import javax.swing.*;** .

A class must be created to represent the GUI to which components can be added to build the interface. This is easily achieved by declaring it a subclass of Swing's **JFrame** class using the **extends** keyword – thereby inheriting attributes and behaviors that allow the user to move, resize, and close the window.

The class constructor should include statements to set these minimum requirements:

● The title of the window – specified as a **String** argument to the inherited **super()** method of the **JFrame** class

● The size of the window – specified as width and height in pixels as arguments to its **setSize()** method

● What to do when the user closes the window – specified as a constant argument to its **setDefaultCloseOperation()** method

● Display the window – specified as a Boolean argument to its **setVisible()** method

Additionally, the constructor can add a **JPanel** container component to the window, in which smaller components can be added, using the inherited **add()** method of the **JFrame** class.

By default, a **JPanel** container employs a **FlowLayout** layout manager that lays out components in left-to-right lines, wrapping at the right edge of the window.

The steps opposite describe how to create a basic window containing a **JPanel** container with a **FlowLayout** layout manager. This window is featured in subsequent examples in this book that demonstrate how to add various components to the **JPanel** container.

Remember the letter **x** in **javax.swing** by thinking of **JAVA** eXtra.

Layout managers are described in more detail on page 148.

...cont'd

1 Start a new program that imports all Swing components
import javax.swing.* ;

Window.java

2 Create a subclass of the **JFrame** class named "Window" containing the standard main method
```
class Window extends JFrame
{
        public static void main ( String[] args ) {          }
}
```

3 Before the main method, create a **JPanel** container object
JPanel pnl = new JPanel( ) ;

4 Next, insert this constructor method to specify window requirements and to add the **JPanel** object to the **JFrame**
```
public Window()
{
        super( "Swing Window" ) ;
        setSize( 500 , 200 ) ;
        setDefaultCloseOperation( EXIT_ON_CLOSE ) ;
        add( pnl ) ;
        setVisible( true ) ;
}
```

Don't forget

The **EXIT_ON_CLOSE** operation is a constant member of the **JFrame** class. It exits the program when the window gets closed.

135

5 Create an instance of the Window class by inserting this line into the main method
Window gui = new Window() ;

6 Save the program as **Window.java** then compile and run the program to see the basic window appear

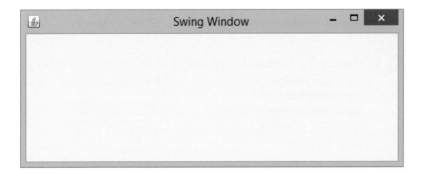

Swing Window

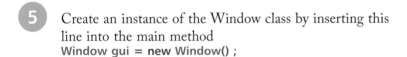

Hot tip

Notice how the **add()** method is used here to add the **JPanel** object to the **JFrame** window.

Adding push buttons

The Swing **JButton** class creates a push button component that can be added to a graphical interface. This lets the user interact with the program by clicking on a button to perform an action.

The **JButton** object is created with the **new** keyword and its constructor takes a **String** argument specifying text to be displayed on that button.

Images can appear on buttons too. An **ImageIcon** object must first be created to represent the image, specifying the image file name as the argument to its constructor. Typically, the image will be located alongside the program but the argument can include the path for images outside the local directory.

Specify the name of the **ImageIcon** object as the argument to the **JButton** constructor to display that image on the button, or specify a **String** and **ImageIcon** as its two arguments to display both text and the image.

Hot tip

Details of how to create event-handler methods to respond to user actions, such as a button click, can be found in the next chapter.

Buttons.java

Don't forget

The **JPanel** object has an **add()** method – to add components to that panel.

1. Edit a copy of **Window.java** from page 135, changing the class name in the declaration, the constructor, and the instance statement from "Window" to "Buttons"

2. Before the **Buttons()** constructor, create two **ImageIcon** objects
   ```
   ImageIcon tick = new ImageIcon( "tick.png" ) ;
   ImageIcon cross = new ImageIcon( "cross.png" ) ;
   ```

3. Next, create three **JButton** objects to display text, an image, and both text and an image respectively
   ```
   JButton btn = new JButton( "Click Me" ) ;
   JButton tickBtn = new JButton( tick ) ;
   JButton crossBtn = new JButton( "STOP" , cross ) ;
   ```

4. Inside the **Buttons()** constructor, insert three statements to add the **JButton** components to the **JPanel** container
   ```
   pnl.add( btn ) ;
   pnl.add( tickBtn ) ;
   pnl.add( crossBtn ) ;
   ```

5. Save the program as **Buttons.java** then compile and run the program to see push buttons appear in the window

...cont'd

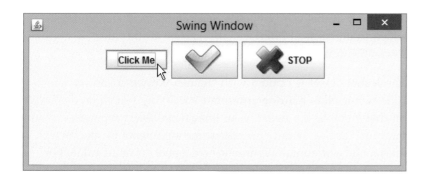

The buttons respond graphically when they are clicked but will not perform an action until the program provides an event-handler method to respond to each click event.

Where the program is intended for deployment in a single Java archive (JAR), image resources must be loaded by a **ClassLoader** object before creating the **ImageIcon** objects to represent them.

Specifying the resource file name or path to the **getResource()** method of a **ClassLoader** returns a URL, which can be used as the argument to the **ImageIcon** constructor. The **java.net** package provides a useful **URL** class to which these may first be assigned.

Details of how to create a Java Archive (JAR) can be found on page 174.

6 Before the **Buttons()** constructor create a **ClassLoader** object
```
ClassLoader ldr = this.getClass().getClassLoader() ;
```

7 Load the URLs of the image resources
```
java.net.URL tickURL = ldr.getResource( "tick.png" ) ;
java.net.URL crossURL = ldr.getResource( "cross.png" ) ;
```

8 Edit the **ImageIcon()** constructors in step 2 to use URLs
```
ImageIcon tick = new ImageIcon( tickURL ) ;
ImageIcon cross = new ImageIcon( crossURL ) ;
```

9 Save the changes then recompile and re-run the program – it will run as before but can now be deployed in a JAR

Notice how the **getClass()** method and **this** keyword are used here to reference this class object.

137

Adding labels

The Swing **JLabel** class creates a label component that can be added to a graphical interface. This can be used to display non-interactive text or image, or both text and an image.

The **JLabel** object is created with the **new** keyword and its constructor takes a **String** argument specifying text to be displayed on that label, or the name of an **ImageIcon** object representing an image to display. It can also take three arguments to specify text, image, and horizontal alignment as a **JLabel** constant value. For example, **JLabel("text", img, JLabel.CENTER)** aligns centrally.

Where a **JLabel** object contains both text and an image the relative position of the text can be determined by specifying a **JLabel** constant as the argument to **setVerticalPosition()** and **setHorizontalPosition()** methods of the **JLabel** object.

Additionally, a **JLabel** object can be made to display a ToolTip when the cursor hovers over, by specifying a text **String** as the argument to that object's **setToolTipText()** method.

Labels.java

1 Edit a copy of **Window.java** from page 135, changing the class name in the declaration, the constructor, and the instance statement from "Window" to "Labels"

2 Before the **Labels()** constructor, create an **ImageIcon** object
ImageIcon duke = new ImageIcon("duke.png") ;

3 Next, create three **JLabel** objects to display an image, text, and both text and an image respectively
JLabel lbl1 = new JLabel(duke) ;
JLabel lbl2 = new JLabel("Duke is the friendly mascot
                    of Java technology.") ;
JLabel lbl3 = new JLabel("Duke" , duke , JLabel.CENTER) ;

4 Inside the **Labels()** constructor insert this statement to create a ToolTip for the first label
lbl1.setToolTipText("Duke - the Java Mascot") ;

5 Add these two statements to align the text centrally below the third label
lbl3.setHorizontalTextPosition(JLabel.CENTER) ;
lbl3.setVerticalTextPosition(JLabel.BOTTOM) ;

6 Now, add three statements to add the the **JLabel** components to the **JPanel** container
```
pnl.add( lbl1 ) ;
pnl.add( lbl2 ) ;
pnl.add( lbl3 ) ;
```

7 Save the program as **Labels.java** then compile and run the program, placing the cursor over the first label

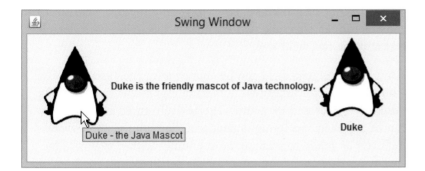

JLabel alignment constants include **LEFT**, **CENTER**, **RIGHT**, **TOP** and **BOTTOM**.

Where the program is intended for deployment in a single Java archive (JAR), the image resource must be loaded by a **ClassLoader** object before creating the **ImageIcon** object to represent it.

Specifying the resource file name or path to the **getResource()** method of a **ClassLoader** returns a URL which can be used as the argument to the **ImageIcon** constructor.

8 Before the **Labels()** constructor create a **ClassLoader** object
```
ClassLoader ldr = this.getClass().getClassLoader() ;
```

9 Edit the **ImageIcon()** constructor in step 2 to load the URL of the image resource using the **ClassLoader** object
```
ImageIcon duke =
        new ImageIcon( ldr.getResource( "duke.png" ) ) ;
```

Details of how to create a Java Archive (JAR) can be found on page 174.

10 Save the changes then recompile and re-run the program – it will run as before but can now be deployed in a JAR

Adding text fields

The Swing **JTextField** class creates a single-line text field component that can be added to a graphical interface. This can be used to display editable text and allows the user to enter text to interact with the program.

The **JTextField** object is created with the **new** keyword and its constructor can take a **String** argument specifying default text to be displayed in that field. In this case, the component will be sized to accommodate the length of the **String**. Alternatively, the argument may be a numeric value to specify the text field size. The constructor can also take two arguments specifying both default text and the text field size.

A multiple-line text field can be created with the **JTextArea** class whose constructor takes two numerical arguments specifying its number of lines and its width. Alternatively, three arguments can be supplied specifying default text, line number, and width. Text can be made to wrap at word endings within this field by specifying **true** as the argument to the **setLineWrap()** method and **setWrapStyleWord()** method of the **JTextArea** object.

Where text entered into a **JTextArea** component exceeds its initial size the component will expand to accommodate the text. To make the component a fixed size with scrolling capability it can be placed in a **JScrollPane** container. This is created with the **new** keyword and takes the name of the **JTextArea** as its argument.

Scroll bars will, by default, only appear when the field contains text that exceeds its initial size – but they can be made to appear constantly by specifying a **JScrollPane** constant as the argument to the snappily named **setVerticalScrollBarPolicy()** or **setHorizontalScrollBarPolicy()** methods of the **JScrollPane** object. For example, to always display a vertical scrollbar use the **JScrollPane.VERTICAL_SCOLLBAR_ALWAYS** constant as the argument.

Hot tip

Use the **JPasswordField** class instead of the **JTextField** class where input characters are needed to be not visible.

TextFields.java

1 Edit a copy of **Window.java** from page 135, changing the class name in the declaration, the constructor, and the instance statement from "Window" to "TextFields"

2 Before the **TextFields()** constructor, create two **JTextField** objects
```
JTextField txt1 = new JTextField( 38 ) ;
JTextField txt2 = new JTextField( "Default Text" , 38 ) ;
```

3 Create a **JTextArea** object five lines high
```
JTextArea txtArea = new JTextArea( 5 , 37 ) ;
```

4 Add a **JScrollPane** object – to contain the **JTextArea** created in step 3
```
JScrollPane pane = new JScrollPane( txtArea ) ;
```

5 In the **TextFields()** constructor method, insert statements to enable the **JTextArea** object to wrap at word endings
```
txtArea.setLineWrap( true ) ;
txtArea.setWrapStyleWord( true ) ;
```

A **JTextArea** component has no scrolling ability unless it is contained within a **JScrollPane** component.

6 Insert a statement to always display a vertical scrollbar for the **JTextArea** object
```
pane.setVerticalScrollBarPolicy
        ( JScrollPane.VERTICAL_SCROLLBAR_ALWAYS ) ;
```

7 Insert two statements to add the the **JTextField** components to the **JPanel** container
```
pnl.add( txt1 ) ;
pnl.add( txt2 ) ;
```

8 Insert another statement to add the **JScrollPane** container, (containing the **JTextArea** field) to the **JPanel** container
```
pnl.add( pane ) ;
```

9 Save the program as **TextFields.java** then compile and run the program, entering some text into the text area

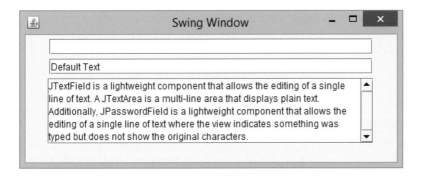

Adding item selectors

The Swing **JCheckBox** class creates a checkbox component that can be added to a graphical interface. This can be used to allow the user to select or deselect individual items in a program. The **JCheckBox** object is created with the **new** keyword and its constructor takes a **String** argument specifying text to be displayed alongside that checkbox. It can also take a second **true** argument to make the checkbox be selected by default.

A choice of items can be offered by the **JComboBox** class that creates a dropdown list from which the user can select any single item. This object is created with the **new** keyword and its constructor typically takes the name of a **String** array as its argument. Each element in the array provides an item for selection in the dropdown list. Similarly, a choice of items can be offered by the **JList** class that creates a fixed-size list from which the user can select one or more items. It is created with the **new** keyword and its constructor also takes an array as its argument, with each element providing an item for selection. As both **JList** and **JComboBox** are "Collections" they must specify the generic type they may contain when they get created, such as **<String>**.

Items.java

1 Edit a copy of **Window.java** from page 135, changing the class name in the declaration, the constructor, and the instance statement from "Window" to "Items"

2 Before the **Items()** constructor create a **String** array of items for selection
```
String[] toppings =
    { "Pepperoni" , "Mushroom" , "Ham" , "Tomato" } ;
```

3 Next, create four **JCheckBox** objects to present each array item for selection – with one selected by default
```
JCheckBox chk1 = new JCheckBox( toppings[0] ) ;
JCheckBox chk2 = new JCheckBox( toppings[1] , true ) ;
JCheckBox chk3 = new JCheckBox( toppings[2] ) ;
JCheckBox chk4 = new JCheckBox( toppings[3] ) ;
```

4 Add a second **String** array of items for selection
```
String[] styles =
    { "Deep Dish" , "Gourmet Style" , "Thin & Crispy" } ;
```

5 Create a **JComboBox** object to present each item in the second array for selection
```
JComboBox<String> box1 =
       new JComboBox<String>( styles ) ;
```

6 Add a **JList** object to present each item in the first array for selection from a list
```
JList<String> lst1 = new JList<String>( toppings ) ;
```

7 In the **Items()** constructor method, insert statements to add each **JCheckBox** component to the **JPanel** container
```
pnl.add( chk1 ) ;
pnl.add( chk2 ) ;
pnl.add( chk3 ) ;
pnl.add( chk4 ) ;
```

8 Insert statements to make a default selection and to add the **JComboBox** component to the **JPanel** container
```
box1.setSelectedIndex( 0 ) ;
pnl.add( box1 ) ;
```

9 Now, insert a statement to add the **JList** component to the **JPanel** container
```
pnl.add( lst1 ) ;
```

10 Save the program as **Items.java** then compile and run the program, selecting items from the lists

Only one item can be selected from a **JComboBox** component – multiple items can be selected from a **JList** component.

143

Details of how to create event-handler methods to respond to user actions, such as an item selection, can be found in the next chapter.

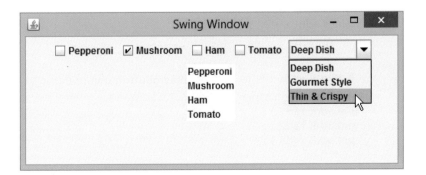

Adding radio buttons

The Swing **JRadioButton** class creates a radio button component that can be added to a graphical interface. This can be used to allow the user to select an item from a group of radio buttons.

The **JRadioButton** object is created with the **new** keyword and its constructor takes a **String** argument specifying text to be displayed alongside that radio button. It can also take a second **true** argument to make a radio button be selected by default.

A **ButtonGroup** object logically groups a number of radio buttons so that only one button in that group can be selected at any time. Each radio button is added to the **ButtonGroup** object by specifying its name as the argument to the group's **add()** method.

Radios.java

The **ButtonGroup** object only groups the buttons logically, not physically.

1 Edit a copy of **Window.java** from page 135, changing the class name in the declaration, the constructor, and the instance statement from "Window" to "Radios"

2 Before the **Radios()** constructor, create three **JRadioButton** objects – with one selected by default
JRadioButton rad1 = new JRadioButton("Red" , true) ;
JRadioButton rad2 = new JRadioButton("Rosé") ;
JRadioButton rad3 = new JRadioButton("White") ;

3 Next, create a **ButtonGroup** object with which to group the radio buttons
ButtonGroup wines = new ButtonGroup() ;

4 In the **Radios()** constructor method, insert statements to add each **JRadioButton** component to the **JButtonGroup**
wines.add(rad1) ;
wines.add(rad2) ;
wines.add(rad3) ;

5 Insert statements to add the **JRadioButton** components to the **JPanel** container
pnl.add(rad1) ;
pnl.add(rad2) ;
pnl.add(rad3) ;

6 Save the program as **Radios.java** then compile and run the program, selecting any one radio button after the default

The examples on the previous pages have demonstrated the most common Swing components – **JButton, JLabel, JTextField, JCheckBox, JComboBox, JList** and **JRadioButton**. There are many more specialized components available in the **javax.swing** package whose details can be found in the Java documentation. For example, the **JSlider, JProgressBar**, and **JMenuBar** components below:

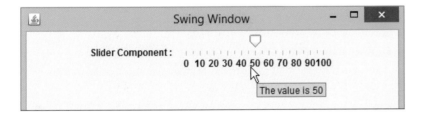

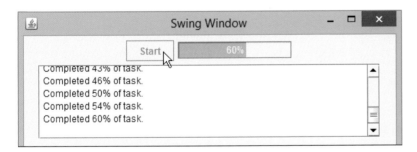

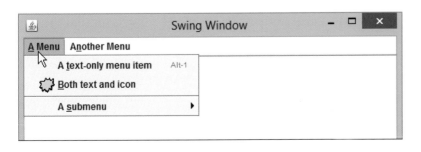

Changing appearance

The **java.awt** package (Abstract Window Toolkit) contains "painting" classes that can be used to color interface components. These can be made available to a program by including the initial statement **import java.awt.*** ; .

Included in the **java.awt** package is a **Color** class that has constants representing a few basic colors, such as **Color.RED**. Additionally, instances of the **Color** class can be created using the **new** keyword to represent custom colors. The constructor can take three integer arguments between zero and 255 to represent red, green, and blue (RGB) values to form the custom color.

Each component has a **setBackground()** method and a **setForeground()** method that take a **Color** object as their argument to paint that component with the specified color.

Note that the background of **JLabel** components are transparent by default so it is recommended that their **setOpaque()** method should be called to set the opacity to **true** before they are painted.

Also in the **java.awt** package is a **Font** class that can be used to modify the font displaying text. A **Font** object represents a font and its constructor can take three arguments to specify name, style and size:

- The specified name should be one of the three platform-independent names "Serif", "SansSerif" or "Monospaced"

- The specified style should be one of the three constants **Font.PLAIN, Font.BOLD** or **Font.ITALIC**

- The specified size should be an integer of the point size

Each component has a **setFont()** method that takes a **Font** object as its argument to paint that component with the specified font.

Custom.java

1 Edit a copy of **Window.java** from page 135, changing the class name in the declaration, the constructor, and the instance statement from "Window" to "Custom"

2 Add a statement at the very start of the program to import the functionality of all classes in the **java.awt** package
import java.awt.* ;

3 Before the **Custom()** constructor create three **JLabel** objects
JLabel lbl1 = new JLabel(**"Custom Background"**) ;
JLabel lbl2 = new JLabel(**"Custom Foreground"**) ;
JLabel lbl3 = new JLabel(**"Custom Font"**) ;

4 Create a **Color** object
Color customColor = new Color(**255** , **0** , **0**) ;

5 Create a **Font** object
Font customFont = new Font(**"Serif"** , Font.PLAIN , **32**) ;

6 In the **Custom()** constructor method, insert statements to
color a **JLabel** background using a **Color** constant
lbl1.setOpaque(**true**) ;
lbl1.setBackground(Color.YELLOW) ;

7 Insert a statement to color a **JLabel** foreground using a
custom **Color** object
lbl2.setForeground(customColor) ;

8 Insert a statement to paint text on a **JLabel** component
using a custom font
lbl3.setFont(customFont) ;

9 Add each label to the **JPanel** container
pnl.add(lbl1) ; pnl.add(lbl2) ; pnl.add(lbl3) ;

10 Save the program as **Custom.java** then compile and run
the program to see the effect

In this case, the custom color is equivalent to **Color.RED** as the RGB value specifies the maximum red value with no green or blue.

147

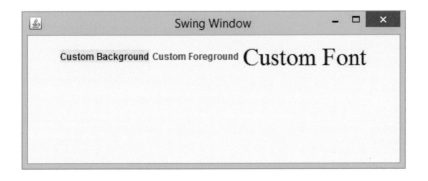

Arranging components

The **java.awt** package (Abstract Window Toolkit) contains a number of layout manager classes that can be used to place components in a container in different ways.

A layout manager object is created using the **new** keyword and can then be specified as the argument to a **JPanel** constructor to have the panel use that layout. When components get added to the panel they will be placed according to the rules of the specified layout manager:

Layout Manager:	Rules:
BorderLayout	Places North, South, East, West and Center (the content pane default)
BoxLayout	Places in a single row or column
CardLayout	Places different components in a specified area at different times
FlowLayout	Places left to right in a wrapping line (the JPanel default)
GridBagLayout	Places in a grid of cells, allowing components to span cells
GridLayout	Places in a grid of rows and columns
GroupLayout	Places horizontally and vertically
SpringLayout	Places by relative spacing

Don't forget

You can find further details of each layout manager in the **java.awt** section of the Java documentation.

148

The top level **JFrame** object has a "content pane" container that places components using the **BorderLayout** layout manager by default. This can be used to place up to five **JPanel** containers, which may each use their default **FlowLayout** layout manager, or any of the layout managers in the table above. Using a variety of layout managers accommodates most layout requirements.

The content pane can be represented by a **java.awt.Container** object, whose **add()** method can specify the position and name of a component to be placed within the content pane.

...cont'd

1 Edit a copy of **Window.java** from page 135, changing the class declaration, constructor, and instance from "Window" to "Layout", then add a statement at the start of the program to import the functionality of the **java.awt** package
import java.awt.* ;

JAVA
Layout.java

2 Before the **Layout()** constructor, create a **Container** object representing the **JFrame** content pane container
Container contentPane = getContentPane() ;

3 Create a second **JPanel** object using a **GridLayout** layout manager in a 2 x 2 grid
JPanel grid = new JPanel(new GridLayout(2 , 2)) ;

4 In the **Layout()** constructor method, insert statements adding **JButton** components to both **JPanel** objects
pnl.add(new JButton("Yes")) ;
pnl.add(new JButton("No")) ;
pnl.add(new JButton("Cancel")) ;
grid.add(new JButton("1")) ;
grid.add(new JButton("2")) ;
grid.add(new JButton("3")) ;
grid.add(new JButton("4")) ;

5 Now, insert statements adding both panels and a button to the content pane
contentPane.add("North" , pnl) ;
contentPane.add("Center" , grid) ;
contentPane.add("West" , new JButton("West")) ;

6 Save the program as **Layout.java** then compile and run the program to see the component layout

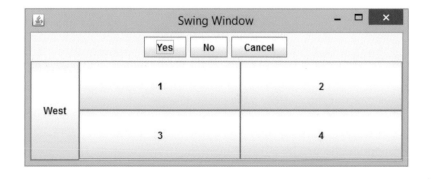

Beware

While the **FlowLayout** maintains the **JButton** size other layout managers expand the components to fill their layout design.

Summary

- The **javax.swing** package contains the Java Swing classes that are used to create GUI components

- A window is created as a top-level **JFrame** container

- The **JFrame** constructor should specify the window's title, size, default close operation and visibility

- A **JPanel** container displays smaller components in a wrapping line using its default **FlowLayout** layout manager

- The **JButton** constructor can specify text and images to be displayed on a push button component

- An **ImageIcon** object represents an image to use in the program

- Programs that are to be deployed as a single Java archive (JAR) should use a **ClassLoader** object to specify an image source

- A **JLabel** object displays non-interactive text and image content

- Editable text can be displayed in **JTextField** and **JTextArea** fields

- A **JScrollPane** object provides scrollbars for a **JTextArea** field

- Items for selection can be displayed with **JCheckBox**, **JComboBox** and **JList** components

- A **ButtonGroup** object logically groups a number of **JRadioButton** components so only one can be selected

- Specific RGB colors can be represented by the **Color** class of the **java.awt** package

- The **java.awt** package has a **Font** class that can be used to create objects representing a particular font name, style, and size

- Multiple **JPanel** containers can be added to a **JFrame** container by using the **Container** class of the **java.awt** package to represent the content pane of the **JFrame**

- When creating a **JPanel** container object its argument may optionally specify a layout manager

9 Recognizing events

This chapter demonstrates how to create Java program event-handlers that respond to user interface actions.

Listening for events

A user can interact with a program that provides a graphical user interface (GUI) by performing actions with a mouse, keyboard, or other input device. These actions cause "events" to occur in the interface and making a program respond to them is known as "event-handling".

For a program to recognize user events it needs to have one or more **EventListener** interfaces added from the **java.awt.event** package. These can be made available to the program by adding an initial statement to **import java.awt.event.* ;** .

The desired **EventListener** interface can be included in the class declaration using the **implements** keyword. For example, a class declaration to listen for button clicks might look like this:

class Click extends JFrame implements ActionListener {   }

The Java documentation describes many **EventListener** interfaces that can listen out for different events but the most common ones are listed in the table below, together with a brief description:

EventListener:	Description:
ActionListener	Recognizes action events that occur when a push button is pushed or released
ItemListener	Recognizes item events that occur when a list item gets selected or deselected
KeyListener	Recognizes keyboard events that occur when the user presses or releases a key
MouseListener	Recognizes mouse button actions that occur when the user presses or releases a mouse button, and when the mouse enters or exits a component
MouseMotionListener	Recognizes motion events that occur when the user moves the mouse

Hot tip

Multiple EventListeners can be included after the **implements** keyword as a comma-separated list.

Generating events

Components need to generate events that the **EventListener** interfaces can recognize if they are to be useful. Having added the appropriate **EventListener** to the program, as described opposite, an event generator must be added to the component.

For example, in order to have the program respond to a button click, the **ActionListener** interface is added to the program and the button's **addActionListener()** method must be called, specifying the **this** keyword as its argument. This makes the button generate an event when it gets clicked, which can be recognized by the **ActionListener** interface.

Statements creating a button that generates events look like this:

```
JButton btn = new JButton( "Click Me" ) ;
btn.addActionListener( this ) ;
```

When the user clicks a button that generates an event the **ActionListener** interface recognizes the event and seeks an event-handler method within the program to execute a response.

Each **EventListener** interface has an associated event-handler method that is called when an event is recognized. For example, when a button gets clicked, the **ActionListener** interface calls an associated method named **actionPerformed()** and passes an **ActionEvent** object as its argument.

An **ActionEvent** object contains information about the event and the source component from where it originated. Most usefully, it has a **getSource()** method that identifies the object that generated the event. This can be used to create an appropriate response for that component.

An event-handler method to create a response for a specific button click could look like this:

```
public void actionPerformed( ActionEvent event )
{
        if ( event.getSource() == btn )
        {
                Statements to be executed for this button click event
        }
}
```

Handling button events

A Swing **JButton** component that is set to generate an **ActionEvent** event when it gets clicked can be recognized by the **ActionListener** interface, which will pass the event to its **actionPerformed()** event-handler method. The **ActionEvent** object has a **getSource()** method that identifies the originating component and a **getActionCommand()** method that returns a **String**. This will be the text label for a button component or the content for a text field component.

One response to a button might be to disable a component by calling its **setEnabled()** method with a **false** argument. Conversely, the component can be enabled once more by specifying a **true** argument to its **setEnabled()** method.

Actions.java

1. Edit a copy of **Window.java** from page 135 changing the class name in the declaration, the constructor, and the instance statement from "Window" to "Actions"

2. Add a statement at the very start of the program to import the functionality of all classes in the **java.awt.event** package
   import java.awt.event.* ;

3. Edit the class declaration to add an **ActionListener** interface to the program
   class Actions extends JFrame implements ActionListener

4. Before the **Actions()** constructor, create two **JButton** push buttons and a **JTextArea** text field
   JButton btn1 = new JButton("Button 1") ;
   JButton btn2 = new JButton("Button 2") ;
   JTextArea txtArea = new JTextArea(5 , 38) ;

5. Add the buttons and text area to the **JPanel** container
   pnl.add(btn1) ;
   pnl.add(btn2) ;
   pnl.add(txtArea) ;

6. Insert statements to set the initial state of two components
   btn2.setEnabled(false) ;
   txtArea.setText("Button 2 is Disabled") ;

...cont'd

7 In the **Actions()** constructor, insert statements to make each button generate an **ActionEvent event** when clicked
btn1.addActionListener(this) ;
btn2.addActionListener(this) ;

8 After the constructor method, add an event-handler method for the **ActionListener** interface – to display text identifying which button has been clicked
public void actionPerformed(ActionEvent event)
{
        txtArea.setText(event.getActionCommand()
                    + " Clicked and Disabled") ;
}

The components are declared before the constructor so they are globally accessible to the event-handler method.

9 Insert **if** statements in the event-handler method – executing a specific response to each button click
if (event.getSource() == btn1)
{ btn2.setEnabled(true) ; btn1.setEnabled(false) ;   }

if (event.getSource() == btn2)
{ btn1.setEnabled(true) ; btn2.setEnabled(false) ;   }

10 Save the program as **Actions.java** then compile and run the program, clicking the push buttons

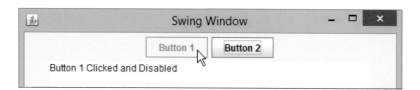

It's sometimes useful to disable a component until the user has performed a required action.

Handling item events

Swing **JRadioButton**, **JCheckBox** and **JComboBox** components maintain states whose change can be recognized by the **ItemListener** interface, which will pass the **ItemEvent** to its **itemStateChanged()** event-handler method. The **ItemEvent** object has a **getItemSelectable()** method that identifies the originating component and a **getStateChange()** method that returns its status. This will determine if the change is selecting or deselecting an item and can be compared to an **ItemEvent.SELECTED** constant.

States.java

1 Edit a copy of **Window.java** from page 135 changing the class name in the declaration, the constructor, and the instance statement from "Window" to "States". Then add a statement at the very start of the program to import the functionality of the **java.awt.event** package
import java.awt.event.* ;

2 Edit the class declaration to add an **ItemListener** interface to the program
class States extends JFrame implements ItemListener

3 Before the **States()** constructor, create these components
String[] styles =
    { "Deep Dish" , "Gourmet Style" , "Thin & Crispy" } ;
JComboBox<String> box =
    new JComboBox<String> (styles) ;
JRadioButton rad1 = new JRadioButton("White") ;
JRadioButton rad2 = new JRadioButton("Red") ;
ButtonGroup wines = new ButtonGroup() ;
JCheckBox chk = new JCheckBox("Pepperoni") ;
JTextArea txtArea = new JTextArea(5 , 38) ;

4 In the **States()** constructor, insert statements to group the two **JRadioButton** components
wines.add(rad1) ;
wines.add(rad2) ;

5 Insert statements to add the components to the **JPanel** container
pnl.add(rad1) ;
pnl.add(rad2) ;
pnl.add(chk) ;
pnl.add(box) ;
pnl.add(txtArea) ;

Hot tip

Note how this example uses the **append()** method to add further text to the text area.

...cont'd

6 Insert statements to make selectable components generate
an **ItemEvent** event when an item is selected or deselected
rad1.addItemListener(this) ;
rad2.addItemListener(this) ;
chk.addItemListener(this) ;
box.addItemListener(this) ;

7 After the constructor method, add an event-handler
method for the **ItemListener** interface – identifying items
selected by the **JRadioButton** components
public void itemStateChanged(ItemEvent event)
{
        if (event.getItemSelectable() == rad1)
        txtArea.setText("White wine selected") ;

        if (event.getItemSelectable() == rad2)
        txtArea.setText("Red wine selected") ;
}

8 Add an **if** statement to the event-handler method to
indicate the status of the **JCheckBox** component
if ((event.getItemSelectable() == chk) &&
  (event.getStateChange() == ItemEvent.SELECTED))
txtArea.append("\nPepperoni selected\n") ;

9 Add an **if** statement to the event-handler method to
indicate the status of the **JComboBox** component
if ((event.getItemSelectable() == box) &&
  (event.getStateChange() == ItemEvent.SELECTED))
txtArea.append(event.getItem().toString() + " selected") ;

10 Save the program as **States.java** then compile and run the
program, selecting various items from left to right

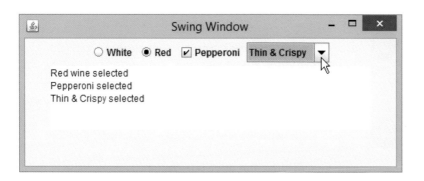

The **JComboBox** fires
two ItemEvents when
an item gets selected –
one selecting the item
and one deselecting
the previously selected
item. That is why steps
8 & 9 must identify
both the originating
component and the type
of **ItemEvent**.

157

Notice that the **getItem()**
method returns the item
affected by the change.

Reacting to keyboard events

Swing components that allow the user to input text can recognize user key strokes with the **KeyListener** interface, which will pass the **KeyEvent** event to these three event-handler methods:

Event-handler:	Description:
keyPressed(KeyEvent)	Called when a key is pressed
keyTyped(KeyEvent)	Called after a key is pressed
keyReleased(KeyEvent)	Called when a key is released

When a program implements the **KeyListener** interface it must declare these three methods – even if not all are actually used.

The **KeyEvent** object has a **getKeyChar()** method, which returns the character for that key, and a **getKeyCode()** method, which returns an integer Unicode value representing that key. Additionally, a **getKeyText()** method takes the key code value as its argument and returns a description of that key.

Keystrokes.java

1 Edit a copy of **Window.java** from page 135 changing the class name in the declaration, the constructor, and the instance statement from "Window" to "Keystrokes". Then add an initial statement to import the functionality of the **java.awt.event** package
import java.awt.event.* ;

2 Edit the class declaration to add a **KeyListener** interface to the program
class Keystrokes extends JFrame implements KeyListener

3 Before the **Keystrokes()** constructor, create a **JTextField** component and a **JTextArea** component
JTextField field = new JTextField(38) ;
JTextArea txtArea = new JTextArea(5 , 38) ;

4 Insert statements to add these two components to the **JPanel** container
pnl.add(field) ; pnl.add(txtArea) ;

158

5 In the **Keystrokes()** constructor, insert a statement to make the **JTextField** component generate **KeyEvent** events
```
field.addKeyListener( this ) ;
```

6 After the constructor method, add an event-handler that acknowledges when a key gets pressed
```
public void keyPressed( KeyEvent event )
{
        txtArea.setText( "Key Pressed" ) ;
}
```

7 Add a second event-handler that displays the key character after the key has been pressed
```
public void keyTyped( KeyEvent event )
{
        txtArea.append( "\nCharacter : "
                                + event.getKeyChar() ) ;
}
```

8 Add a third event-handler that displays the key code and key text when the key gets released
```
public void keyReleased( KeyEvent event )
{
        int keyCode = event.getKeyCode() ;
        txtArea.append( "\nKey Code : "
                                + event.getKeyCode() ) ;
        txtArea.append( "\nKey Text : "
                                + event.getKeyText( keyCode ) ) ;
}
```

9 Save the program as **Keystrokes.java** then compile and run the program, typing in the top text field

The **getKeyCode()** method only returns the key code if called from within the **keyPressed()** or **keyReleased()** event-handlers – not from the **keyTyped()** event-handler.

Run this program and press a non-character key, such as Backspace, to see its key text name.

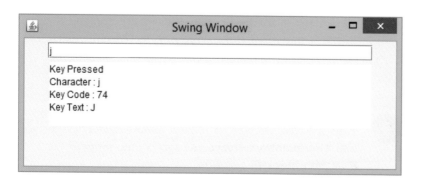

159

Responding to mouse events

Swing components can recognize user mouse actions with the **MouseListener** interface, which will pass the **MouseEvent** event to these five event-handler methods:

Event-handler:	Description:
mousePressed(MouseEvent)	Button is pressed
mouseReleased(MouseEvent)	Button is released
mouseClicked(MouseEvent)	Button has been released
mouseEntered(MouseEvent)	Mouse moves on
mouseExited(MouseEvent)	Mouse moves off

Mouse movements can be recognized by the **MouseMotionListener** interface, which passes **MouseEvent** events to two event-handlers:

Event-handler:	Description:
mouseMoved(MouseEvent)	Mouse is moved
mouseDragged(MouseEvent)	Mouse is dragged

When a program implements the **MouseListener** or **MouseMotionListener** interface it must declare all its associated event-handler methods – even if not all are actually used.

The **MouseEvent** object passed by the **MouseMotionListener** interface has **getX()** and **getY()** methods, which returns the current mouse coordinates relative to the component generating the event.

Mouse.java

1 Edit a copy of **Window.java** from page 135 changing the class name in the declaration, the constructor, and the instance statement from "Window" to "Mouse". Then add an initial statement to import the functionality of the **java.awt.event** package
import java.awt.event.* ;

2 Edit the class declaration to add a **MouseListener** interface and **MouseMotionListener** interface to the program
class Mouse extends JFrame
            implements MouseListener , MouseMotionListener

3 Before the **Mouse()** constructor, create a **JTextArea** component and two integer variables to store coordinates

```
JTextArea txtArea = new JTextArea( 8 , 38 ) ;
int x , y ;
```

4 In the **Mouse()** constructor, insert statements to add the **JTextArea** component to the **JPanel** container and to make it generate **MouseEvent** events

```
pnl.add( txtArea ) ;
txtArea.addMouseMotionListener( this ) ;
txtArea.addMouseListener( this ) ;
```

Hot tip

Rollover effects can be created by swapping images with the **mouseEntered()** and **mouseExited()** event-handler methods.

5 After the constructor method, add the two event-handlers for the **MouseMotionListener** interface

```
public void mouseMoved( MouseEvent event )
{ x = event.getX() ; y = event.getY() ;    }
public void mouseDragged( MouseEvent event ) { }
```

6 Add five event-handlers for the **MouseListener** interface

```
public void mouseEntered( MouseEvent event )
{ txtArea.setText( "\nMouse Entered" ) ;          }

public void mousePressed( MouseEvent event )
{ txtArea.append( "\nMouse Pressed at X: " +x+ "Y: " +y ) ; }

public void mouseReleased( MouseEvent event )
{ txtArea.append( "\nMouse Released" ) ;          }

public void mouseClicked(MouseEvent event ) {  }
public void mouseExited(MouseEvent event )  {  }
```

7 Save the program as **Mouse.java** then compile and run the program, clicking on the **JTextArea** component

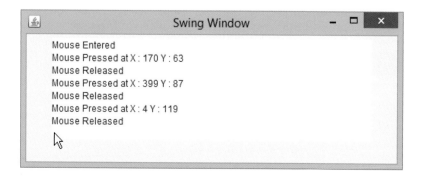

Announcing messages

The Swing **JOptionPane** class is designed to create a standard dialog box centered on its parent window. Its **showMessageDialog()** method displays a message to the user providing information, warning, or error description.

The **showMessageDialog()** method can take four arguments:

- Parent object – typically referenced by the **this** keyword

- Message **String** to be displayed

- Dialog title **String**

- One of the **JOptionPane** constants, **INFORMATION_MESSAGE**, **WARNING_MESSAGE**, or **ERROR_MESSAGE**

The dialog box will display an appropriate icon according to which **JOptionPane** constant is specified.

Messages.java

1 Edit a copy of **Window.java** from page 135 changing the class name in the declaration, the constructor, and the instance statement from "Window" to "Messages"

2 Add an initial statement to import the functionality of the **java.awt.event** package
import java.awt.event.* ;

3 Edit the class declaration to add an **ActionListener** interface to the program
class Messages extends JFrame implements ActionListener

4 Before the **Messages()** constructor, create three **JButton** components
JButton btn1= new JButton("Show Information Message") ;
JButton btn2= new JButton("Show Warning Message") ;
JButton btn3= new JButton("Show Error Message") ;

5 Insert statements to add the button components to the **JPanel** container
pnl.add(btn1) ;
pnl.add(btn2) ;
pnl.add(btn3) ;

...cont'd

6 In the **Messages()** constructor, insert statements to make
each button generate an **ActionEvent** event
btn1.addActionListener(this) ;
btn2.addActionListener(this) ;
btn3.addActionListener(this) ;

7 After the constructor method, add an event-handler
method for the **ActionListener** interface
public void actionPerformed(ActionEvent event) {   }

Hot tip

You can also simply
specify the parent
and message as two
arguments to create a
dialog with the default
information icon and the
default "Message" title.

8 Between the curly brackets of the event-handler insert **if**
statements to display a dialog when a button gets clicked
if (event.getSource() == btn1)
JOptionPane.showMessageDialog(this , "Information..." ,
"Message Dialog", JOptionPane.INFORMATION_MESSAGE) ;

if (event.getSource() == btn2)
JOptionPane.showMessageDialog(this , "Warning..." ,
"Message Dialog" , JOptionPane.WARNING_MESSAGE) ;

if (event.getSource() == btn3)
JOptionPane.showMessageDialog(this , "Error..." ,
"Message Dialog" , JOptionPane.ERROR_MESSAGE) ;

9 Save the program as **Messages.java** then compile and run
the program, clicking on each button

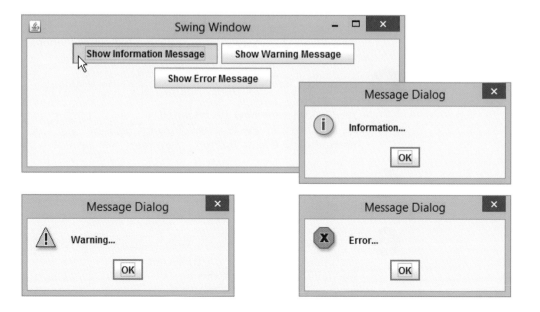

Requesting input

The Swing **JOptionPane** class can request information from the user by opening a dialog box with its **showConfirmationDialog()** method, requesting a decison, or with its **showInputDialog()** method, requesting user input.

Both these methods can take four arguments:

● Parent object – typically referenced by the **this** keyword

● Request **String** to be displayed

● Dialog title **String**

● One of the **JOptionPane** constants such as **PLAIN_MESSAGE**, or to specify dialog decision buttons as **YES_NO_CANCEL_OPTION**

The dialog box will return the input **String** from an input dialog or an integer from a decision button – zero for yes, 1 for no, or 2 for cancel.

Request.java

1 Edit a copy of **Window.java** from page 135 changing the class name in the declaration, the constructor, and the instance statement from "Window" to "Request". Then add an initial statement to import the functionality of the **java.awt.event** package
import java.awt.event.* ;

2 Edit the class declaration to add an **ActionListener** interface to the program
class Request extends JFrame implements ActionListener

3 Before the **Request()** constructor, create a **JTextField** and two **JButton** components
JTextField field = new JTextField(38) ;
JButton btn1 = new JButton("Request Decision") ;
JButton btn2 = new JButton("Request Input") ;

4 Add each component to the **JPanel** container
pnl.add(field) ; pnl.add(btn1) ; pnl.add(btn2) ;

5 In the **Request()** constructor, insert statements to make each button generate an **ActionEvent** event
btn1.addActionListener(this) ;
btn2.addActionListener(this) ;

6 After the constructor method, add an event-handler method for the **ActionListener** interface
```
public void actionPerformed( ActionEvent event ) {        }
```

7 Between the curly brackets of the event-handler, insert an **if** statement to respond to a decison button click
```
if ( event.getSource() == btn1 )
{
        int n = JOptionPane.showConfirmDialog( this ,
                "Do you agree?" , "Confirmation Dialog" ,
                JOptionPane.YES_NO_CANCEL_OPTION ) ;
        switch( n )
        {
                case 0 : field.setText( "Agreed" ) ; break ;
                case 1 : field.setText( "Disagreed" ) ; break ;
                case 2 : field.setText( "Cancelled" ) ; break ;
        }
}
```

Hot tip

The **OK_CANCEL** constant provides two decision buttons – **OK** returns zero and **CANCEL** returns 2. Refer to the documentation for the full range of constants.

8 Insert an **if** statement to handle user input
```
if ( event.getSource() == btn2 )
field.setText( JOptionPane.showInputDialog( this ,
                "Enter your comment" , "Input Dialog" ,
                JOptionPane.PLAIN_MESSAGE ) ) ;
```

9 Save the program as **Request.java** then compile and run the program, clicking on each button

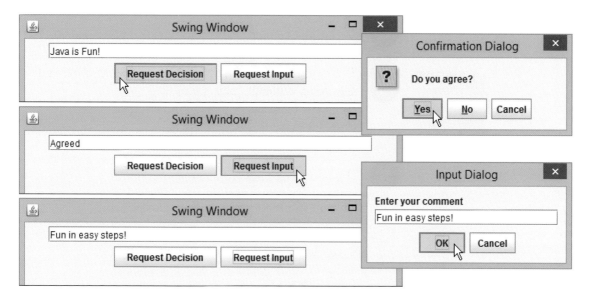

Playing sounds

The **java.applet** package contains a class named **AudioClip** that has methods to play audio files in **.au**, **.aiff**, **.wav** and **.mid** formats. Compatability with Swing components is supported by the Swing **JApplet** class, which provides a **newAudioClip()** method that returns the URL of the audio file.

You can find more on loading image resources with **ClassLoader** on page 139.

The audio file should be loaded as a resource into an **AudioClip** object using the **getResource()** method of a **ClassLoader** object – in the same way that an image resource can be loaded.

Audio playback can be started and stopped in response to user actions with the **play()** and **stop()** methods of the **AudioClip** object. Additionally, the audio file can be played continuously using its **loop()** method.

Sound.java

1. Edit a copy of **Window.java** from page 135 changing the class name in the declaration, the constructor, and the instance statement from "Window" to "Sound"

2. Add an initial statement to import the functionality of all classes in the **java.awt.event** package
   import java.awt.event.* ;

3. Edit the class declaration to add an **ActionListener** interface to the program
   class Sound extends JFrame implements ActionListener

4. Before the **Sound()** constructor create a **ClassLoader** object
   ClassLoader ldr = this.getClass().getClassLoader() ;

music.wav

5. Create an **AudioClip** object and load an audio file resource using the **ClassLoader** object
   java.applet.AudioClip audio =
   JApplet.newAudioClip(ldr.getResource("music.wav")) ;

6. Create two **JButton** components to control audio playback
   JButton playBtn = new JButton("Play") ;
   JButton stopBtn = new JButton("Stop") ;

...cont'd

7 Add the buttons to the **JPanel** container
```
pnl.add( playBtn ) ;
pnl.add( stopBtn ) ;
```

8 In the **Sound()** constructor, insert statements to make each button generate an **ActionEvent** when it gets clicked
```
playBtn.addActionListener( this ) ;
stopBtn.addActionListener( this ) ;
```

Hot tip

Multiple **AudioClip** sounds can be played at the same time.

9 After the constructor method, add an event-handler for the **ActionListener** interface
```
public void actionPerformed( ActionEvent event ) {        }
```

10 Between the curly brackets of the event-handler method, insert a statement to play the audio file when the "Play" button gets clicked
```
if ( event.getSource() == playBtn ) audio.play() ;
```

11 Insert a statement to stop playback of the audio file when the "Stop" button gets clicked
```
if ( event.getSource() == stopBtn ) audio.stop() ;
```

12 Save the program as **Sound.java** then compile and run the program, using the buttons to control audio playback

Don't forget

Each time the **play()** method is called playback starts at the beginning.

Summary

- The **implements** keyword can be used in a class declaration to add one or more **EventListener** interfaces

- A component's **addActionListener()** method takes the **this** keyword as its argument – to make that component generate an **ActionEvent** event when it is activated

- The **ActionListener** interface passes a generated **ActionEvent** event as the argument to its **actionPerformed()** event-handler, which can respond to a push button click made by the user

- The **getSource()** method of an **ActionEvent** event can be used to identify the originating component that generated the event

- An **ItemListener** interface passes a generated **ItemEvent** event as the argument to its **itemStateChanged()** event-handler, which can respond to an item selection made by the user

- The **getItemSelectable()** method of an **ItemEvent** event can be used to identify the component that generated the event

- A **KeyListener** interface passes a generated **KeyEvent** event as the argument to three required event-handler methods, which can respond to a key press and reveal that key's character

- A **MouseListener** interface passes a generated **MouseEvent** event as the argument to five required event-handler methods, which can respond to mouse actions made by the user

- A **MouseMotionListener** interface passes a generated **MouseEvent** event as the argument to two required event-handlers, which can respond to mouse movement

- The **showMessageDialog()** method of the **JOptionPane** class creates a dialog displaying a message to the user, and its **showInputDialog()** and **showConfirmationDialog()** methods can be used to request user input

- Audio resources can be represented by the **AudioClip** class of the **java.applet** package, and played using its **play()** method

10 Deploying programs

This chapter demonstrates how to deploy Java programs – both as desktop applications and as applets embedded in web pages.

Methods of deployment

Java technology provides two separate ways to deploy programs:

- Desktop applications that can be executed on any platform where the appropriate Java Runtime Environment is installed

- Web page applets that can be executed on any web browser upon which the appropriate Java Plugin has been installed

The choice of deployment method is usually determined by the program's purpose. Typically, applets are favored for lightweight programs whose purpose is integrated with web page content, whereas desktop applications are favored for more weighty programs of independent purpose.

Applets and desktop applications can both be created from a common development program – like the **Lotto.java** program listed opposite.

The **Lotto()** constructor builds a simple Swing interface of a single panel containing one label, one text field, and one button. This panel gets loaded into a window frame measuring 260 x 200. The label component merely displays a descriptive graphic image:

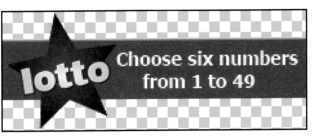

Lotto.png – Checkered areas are transparent

More interestingly, the button's event-handler method executes an algorithm to select a sequence of six random numbers in the range of 1-49 for display in the text field component.

The **Lotto.java** development program, described here, is used throughout this chapter to create both an application and applet.

Beware

Programs in this book are compiled with Java 8 – to run correctly applications require the appropriate Java 8 JRE, and applets require the Java 8 browser plugin.

```java
import javax.swing.* ;
import java.awt.event.* ;

public class Lotto extends JFrame implements ActionListener
{
    // Components.
    ClassLoader ldr = this.getClass().getClassLoader() ;
    java.net.URL iconURL = ldr.getResource( "Lotto.png" ) ;
    ImageIcon icon = new ImageIcon( iconURL ) ;
    JLabel img = new JLabel( icon ) ;
    JTextField txt = new JTextField( "" , 18 ) ;
    JButton btn = new JButton( "Get My Lucky Numbers" ) ;
    JPanel pnl = new JPanel() ;

    // Constructor.
    public Lotto()
    {
        super( "Lotto Application" ) ; setSize( 260 , 200 ) ;
        setDefaultCloseOperation( JFrame.EXIT_ON_CLOSE ) ;
        pnl.add( img ) ; pnl.add( txt ) ; pnl.add( btn ) ;
        btn.addActionListener( this ) ;
        add( pnl ) ; setVisible( true ) ;
    }

    // Event-handler.
    public void actionPerformed( ActionEvent event )
    {
        if ( event.getSource() == btn )
        {
            int[] nums = new int[50] ; String str = "" ;
            for ( int i = 1 ; i < 50 ; i++ ) { nums[i] = i ; }
            for ( int i = 1 ; i < 50 ; i++ )
            {   int r = (int) ( 49 * Math.random() ) + 1 ;
                int temp= nums[i] ; nums[i]= nums[r] ; nums[r]= temp ; }
            for ( int i = 1 ; i < 7 ; i++ )
            {   str += " " + Integer.toString( nums[i] ) + " " ;      }
            txt.setText( str ) ;
        }
    }

    // Entry point.
    public static void main ( String[] args )
    {   Lotto lotto = new Lotto() ;          }
}
```

Lotto.java

Hot tip

The algorithm in this event-handler shuffles integers 1-49 in an array, then assigns those integers in the first six elements to a string.

171

Distributing programs

The **ClassLoader** object in the **Lotto.java** program on the previous page expects the image file resource **Lotto.png** to be located in the same directory as the program file, so the files must be arranged in this way before attempting to compile the program:

Observing the required file arrangement, the **javac** compiler can be employed in the usual way to create a **Lotto.class** file, then the **java** interpreter can be employed to execute the program:

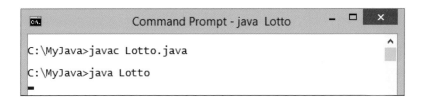

The **Lotto** program opens a new window of the specified size containing the Swing interface components. Each time the user clicks the push button its event-handler displays six new random numbers in the range 1-49 within the text field component:

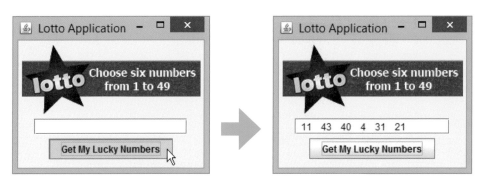

...cont'd

As with all other examples in this book, the example **Lotto** program has been compiled here for Java 8 and can be distributed for execution on other computers where the Java 8 Runtime Environment is present – regardless of their operating system.

For example, in the screenshots below **Lotto.class** and **Lotto.png** files have been copied to the desktop of a computer running the Linux operating system with the Java 8 runtime installed. The **Lotto** program can, therefore, be executed by the **java** interpreter in the same way as on the originating Windows system opposite:

The **.java** source code file need not be included when distributing a program – only **.class** and resource files are needed.

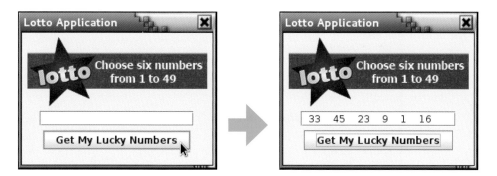

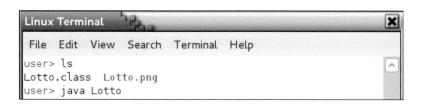

There is, however, a danger in distributing Java programs this way as the program will fail to execute if resource files become unavailable – in this case, removing **Lotto.png** produces this error:

Larger programs may use many resource files whose location can easily be disrupted by a user – the solution, described overleaf, is to package the program and all its resources into a single executable archive file.

173

Building archives

The JDK contains a **jar** utility tool that allows program class and resource files to be bundled into a single Java archive (JAR) file. This compresses all program files, using the popular ZIP format, into a single file with a **.jar** file extension. A JAR file stores the program efficiently and helps ensure that resource files do not become accidentally isolated. The **java** interpreter fully supports JAR files so Java applications and applets can be executed without extracting the individual files. Like the **java** interpreter and **javac** compiler, the **jar** tool is located in Java's **bin** directory and runs from the command line to perform these common **jar** operations:

Hot tip

For larger programs the * wildcard character can be used to archive multiple files within the directory – for instance, **jar cf Program.jar *.class** archives all class files in the current directory.

Command syntax:	Operation:
jar cf *jar-file input-file/s*	Create a JAR file
jar cfe *jar-file entry-point input-file/s*	Create a JAR file with a specified entry point in a standalone application
jar tf *jar-file*	View contents of a JAR file
jar uf *jar-file*	Update contents of JAR file
jar ufm *jar-file attribute-file*	Update contents of JAR file manifest, adding attribute/s
jar xf *jar-file*	Extract all contents of JAR
jar xf *jar-file archived-file/s*	Extract specific files from JAR

Follow these steps to create a JAR file for the Lotto program described at the start of this chapter.

Lotto.jar

1. Open a Command Prompt/Terminal window then navigate to the directory where the Lotto program files are located – **Lotto.class** and **Lotto.png**

2. At the prompt, type **jar cfe Lotto.jar Lotto Lotto.class Lotto.png** then hit Return to create a **Lotto.jar** archive

3. Now, type **jar tf Lotto.jar** to see all contents of the JAR

...cont'd

```
C:\MyJava>jar cfe Lotto.jar Lotto Lotto.class Lotto.png

C:\MyJava>jar tf Lotto.jar
META-INF/
META-INF/MANIFEST.MF
Lotto.class
Lotto.png
```

Notice that the **jar** tool automatically creates a **META-INF** directory alongside the archived files. This contains a text-based manifest meta file named **MANIFEST.MF**. To give applications full access to other resources a "Permissions" attribute line needs to be added to the manifest file by updating the JAR.

4 Launch a plain text edit and precisely type
Application-Name: Lotto
Permissions: all-permissions
– then save the file as **permissions.txt** alongside the JAR

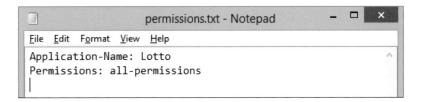

```
permissions.txt - Notepad
File  Edit  Format  View  Help
Application-Name: Lotto
Permissions: all-permissions
|
```

5 At a prompt, type **jar ufm Lotto.jar permissions.txt** then hit Return to add the Permissions attribute to the manifest

```
C:\MyJava>jar ufm Lotto.jar permissions.txt

C:\MyJava>_
```

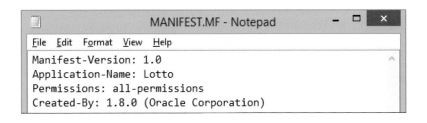

```
MANIFEST.MF - Notepad
File  Edit  Format  View  Help
Manifest-Version: 1.0
Application-Name: Lotto
Permissions: all-permissions
Created-By: 1.8.0 (Oracle Corporation)
```

The **permissions.txt** file must end with newline character – hit return at the end of the final line before saving the file.

permissions.txt

175

Extract a copy of the **META-INF** directory using **jar xf Lotto.jar META-INF** to examine the **MANIFEST.MF** file – it should look like the final illustration shown here.

Deploying applications

Java JAR files are executable on any system on which the appropriate version of the Java Runtime is installed.

At the command line navigate to the directory where the **Lotto.jar** file is located then type **java -jar Lotto.jar** and hit Return to run the Lotto application

Beware

The **.jar** file extension is required when executing JAR files from a prompt.

2 Alternatively, double-click on or right-click the **Lotto.jar** file icon and choose to "Open With" the Java Runtime

Hot tip

Set the JRE as the default JAR file handler on your system for permanent double-click execution.

Signing jars

Java programs that are intended for wider distribution must assure the user they are trustworthy by digitally signing the JAR file. Attempting to launch an unsigned Java application distributed via the internet with Java Web Start or as a Java Applet embedded in a web page will simply produce an error dialog:

Code signing certificates are provided by a trusted Certificate Authority (CA) such as VeriSign, DigiCert, and GlobalSign. These are issued after the CA has verified the authenticity of the developer so the user can be sure of the program's stated source. The CA provides a personal file to the developer containing a private key with which to digitally sign JAR files and the JDK contains a **jarsigner** utility tool for this purpose.

1 Open a Command Prompt/Terminal window then navigate to the directory where **Lotto.jar** is located

2 Enter a **jarsigner** command that identifies the key file, store type, JAR file, and developer name, then hit Return
jarsigner   **-keystore certificate.pfx**
          -storetype pkcs12
          Lotto.jar "Mike McGrath"

3 When prompted enter the keystore passphrase you will have supplied to the CA for this certificate – see the response confirming signature of the JAR file

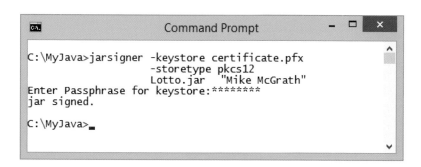

The JDK has a **keytool** utility that can generate self-signed certificates but self-signed JAR files are no longer acceptable.

certificate.pfx
– this file is NOT included in the book's download archive as you will need your own certificate.

You can verify that the JAR has been signed with the command **jarsigner -verify Lotto.jar**.

Enabling Web Start

Java Web Start technology allows a user to launch a Java application by simply clicking on a hyperlink in a web page. The link points to a JNLP (Java Network Launching Protocol) file that provides application information in XML file format. Follow these steps to launch the Lotto application from a web page link:

JNLP

Lotto.jnlp

1 Open a plain text editor, such as Notepad, then copy the following XML content to create a JNLP file

```
<?xml version = "1.0" encoding = "UTF-8" ?>
<jnlp spec = "1.0+"
  codebase = "file:///C:/MyJava/" href = "Lotto.jnlp" >
<information>
  <title>Lotto Application</title>
  <vendor>Java in easy steps</vendor>
  <homepage href = "http://www.ineasysteps.com" />
  <offline-allowed />
</information><security><all-permissions/></security>
<resources>
  <jar href = "Lotto.jar" />
  <j2se version = "1.6+"
        href = "http://java.sun.com/products/autodl/j2se" />
</resources>
<application-desc main-class = "Lotto" />
</jnlp>
```

Hot tip

Remember that the JNLP must set **all-permissions** security – to match those in the JAR file's manifest.

178

HTML

Lotto.html

2 Save the new JNLP file as **Lotto.jnlp** alongside **Lotto.jar**

3 Add an HTML file **Lotto.html** to the same directory and include this hyperlink in its body content
`<a href = "Lotto.jnlp" >Launch the Lotto application</a>`

4 Open **Lotto.html** in your web browser and click the link to launch the Lotto application via Web Start

...cont'd

The Java Web Start splash dialog appears briefly, while the application loads, then the application executes as normal.

To enable Web Start to deliver applications online, the web server must first be configured to support JNLP by recognizing the MIME type of **application/x-java-jnlp-file JNLP**. The JNLP **codebase** atrribute can then be amended to specify the application's location on the server using its HTTP address – for instance, **codebase= "http://www.myserver/java-apps/"**. After uploading the JNLP, JAR and HTML files to that location, Web Start can load the application from the hyperlink as before.

When Web Start first loads an application the information in the JNLP file is automatically stored in the local Java Cache Viewer. This can be used to launch the application again, and to create a convenient desktop shortcut to launch the application.

The **codebase** attribute must accurately specify the file's host directory – or Web Start will be unable to find it and the program will not launch.

1 To open the Java Cache Viewer on Windows, click on the Java icon in Control Panel, then click the View button on the General Tab in the Java Control Panel dialog

2 Select the Lotto program then click the Run button, to launch the application

3 Click the Install Shortcuts button to add a desktop shortcut then click on that to run the Lotto application

The Java Cache Viewer can also be launched from a prompt, on both Windows and Linux systems, by the command **javaws -viewer**

Producing applets

As an alternative to creating programs as Java applications, which are executed by the system's Java Runtime Environment, programs can be produced as embedded web page Java applets, which are executed by the web browser's Java plugin.

Java applets differ from Java applications in two main respects:

- Applets need no window frame – they are allocated space within a web page by HTML code attributes

- Applets have no **main** method – they employ an **init()** method in place of a constructor and the main method

To recognize the full difference follow these steps to convert the **Lotto.java** application, listed on page 171, into an applet:

1   Change the class name from **Lotto** to **LottoApplet** then replace **JFrame** in the class declaration with **JApplet**

2   Change the constructor into an applet **init** method by replacing **public Lotto()** with **public void init()**

3   Remove all statements specifying window features in the former constructor by deleting the following lines
```
super( "Lotto Application" ) ;
setSize( 260 , 200 ) ;
setDefaultCloseOperation( JFrame.EXIT_ON_CLOSE ) ;
setVisible( true ) ;
```

4   Add the ability to set the applet's background color from a hexadecimal parameter value in the HTML code
```
String bgStr = getParameter( "BgColor" ) ;
int bgHex = Integer.parseInt( bgStr , 16 ) ;
pnl.setBackground( new java.awt.Color( bgHex ) );
```

5   Remove the main method by deleting this code block
```
public static void main( String[] args )
{        Lotto lotto = new Lotto() ;        }
```

6   Save the amended file named exactly as **LottoApplet.java** – the content should look just like the listing opposite

Beware

Applet **init** declarations must include the **void** keyword – an applet can't return a value.

```java
import javax.swing.* ;
import java.awt.event.* ;

public class LottoApplet extends JApplet implements ActionListener
{
    // Components.
    ClassLoader ldr = this.getClass().getClassLoader() ;
    java.net.URL iconURL = ldr.getResource( "Lotto.png" ) ;
    ImageIcon icon = new ImageIcon( iconURL ) ;
    JLabel img = new JLabel( icon ) ;
    JTextField txt = new JTextField( "" , 18 ) ;
    JButton btn = new JButton( "Get My Lucky Numbers" ) ;
    JPanel pnl = new JPanel() ;

    // Applet entry point.
    public void init()
    {
        pnl.add( img ) ; pnl.add( txt ) ; pnl.add( btn ) ;
        btn.addActionListener( this ) ;
        String bgStr = getParameter( "BgColor" ) ;
        int bgHex = Integer.parseInt( bgStr , 16 ) ;
        pnl.setBackground( new java.awt.Color( bgHex ) ) ;
        add( pnl ) ;
    }

    // Event-handler.
    public void actionPerformed( ActionEvent event )
    {
        if ( event.getSource() == btn )
        {
            int[] nums = new int[50] ; String str = "" ;
            for ( int i = 1 ; i < 50 ; i++ ) { nums[ i ] = i ; }
            for ( int i = 1 ; i < 50 ; i++ )
            {
                int r = (int) Math.ceil( 49 * Math.random() ) + 1 ;
                int temp=nums[i]; nums[i]=nums[r]; nums[r]=temp;
            }
            for ( int i = 1 ; i < 7 ; i++ )
            {   str += " " + Integer.toString( nums[ i ] ) + " " ;        }
            txt.setText( str ) ;
        }
    }
}
```

LottoApplet.java

The LottoApplet components and event-handler are unchanged from those in the Lotto application.

Converting web pages

In order to embed a Java applet within the contents of a web page, simple HTML code needs to be inserted into the page's source code to allocate a space in which the applet can run.

An opening HTML5 **<object>** tag first describes the object as a Java applet by assigning a value of **"application/x-java-applet"** to its **type** attribute. The applet's size on the web page is then determined by assigning numerical pixel values to its **width** and **height** attributes.

Parameters to be used by the applet are then specified to **name** and **value** attributes of **<param>** tags, which are enclosed between the **<object>** **</object>** tags. There must be one **<param>** tag that assigns a **"code"** term to its **name** attribute and the Java applet filename to its **value** attribute to identify the applet. The **<object>** element may also enclose an optional fallback message to be displayed on the web page when the applet cannot run.

The JDK's **bin** directory contains an **appletviewer** tool that can be used to preview an applet in a specified HTML document.

LottoApplet.html

1 Open a plain text editor, such as Notepad, then copy the following HTML5 content to create an applet host file

```
<!DOCTYPE HTML>
<html>
  <head>
    <meta charset = "UTF-8" >
    <title>Lotto Applet Host</title>
  </head>
  <body>
    <object type = "application/x-java-applet"
        width = "260" height = "160" >
      <param name = "code" value = "LottoApplet.class" >
      <param name = "BgColor" value = "FFFF00" >
      [ Java Applet - Requires Java Plugin ]
    </object>
  </body>
</html>
```

LottoApplet.class

2 Save this as **LottoApplet.html** alongside the program files

3 At a prompt, compile the **LottoApplet.java** program (listed on the previous page) to create the **LottoApplet.class**, then use the JDK **appletviewer** tool to preview the applet

...cont'd

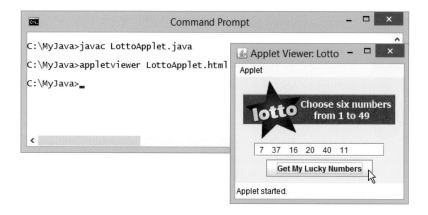

The background of the **LottoApplet.class** applet is set by the HTML **BgColor** parameter (**FFFF00** = Yellow) but otherwise executes exactly as its **Lotto** application counterpart. As with Java applications, it's recommended to package all Java applet files into a single JAR archive so that resource files do not become accidentally isolated – and to keep the applet compact. A further HTML **<param>** element must be added to assign an **"archive"** term to its **name** attribute and JAR filename to its **value** attribute.

4 Insert the tag below within the **<object>** element in **LottoApplet.html** then save the file once more
```
<param name = "archive" value = "LottoApplet.jar" >
```

5 Create a **LottoApplet.jar** archive, containing **Lotto.png** and **LottoApplet.class**, alongside the HTML file – then preview with **appletviewer** again to see it run as before

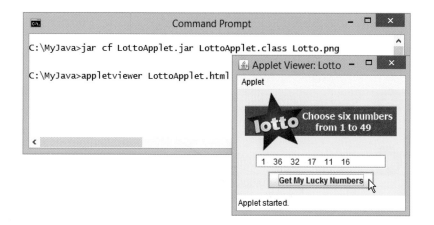

The **code** parameter is still needed in addition to the archive parameter – to indicate the class containing the program entry point.

183

LottoApplet.jar

Deploying applets

As Java applets are intended for wide distribution via the internet the JAR file must be granted permissions and be digitally signed.

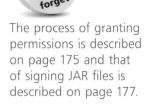

The process of granting permissions is described on page 175 and that of signing JAR files is described on page 177.

1 Type **jar ufm LottoApplet.jar permissions.txt** and hit Return to add the Permissions attribute to the manifest

2 Enter a **jarsigner** command that identifies the key file, store type, JAR file, and developer name, then hit Return
jarsigner   -keystore certificate.pfx
                 -storetype pkcs12
                 LottoApplet.jar "Mike McGrath"

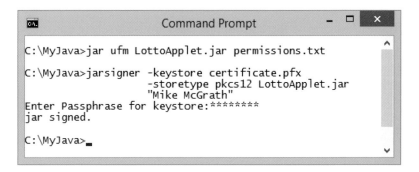

```
C:\MyJava>jar ufm LottoApplet.jar permissions.txt

C:\MyJava>jarsigner -keystore certificate.pfx
                    -storetype pkcs12 LottoApplet.jar
                    "Mike McGrath"
Enter Passphrase for keystore:********
jar signed.

C:\MyJava>_
```

Unexpected problems can arise when viewing applets on different web browsers and platforms so it's a good idea to test an applet in as many environments as you possibly can before deployment.

PlayLotto.html

3 Copy and paste the applet's cross-browser HTML5 code into a desired location on the web page to be deployed

4 Adjust any customizable HTML parameters to suit the deployment page – with **LottoApplet** adjust the hexadecimal **BgColor** parameter to match the background color of its surroundings on the page

5 Save the adjusted web page on your computer then view the changes in your web browser

6 When you are satisfied with the applet's appearance upload the web page and JAR file to your web server, then test its online performance in all environments

Don't forget

Text between the HTML5 **<object>** and **</object>** tags is a fallback message that the browser may choose to display if the applet cannot be loaded.

Web browsers that do not have the Java plugin installed, or do not have Java enabled, may display the specified fallback message on the page in place of the applet. Where Java is enabled the applet will provide the same functionality on the web page as that of the desktop Java application from which the applet is derived:

Hot tip

The LottoApplet background color is adjusted here to match that of the table in which it appears on the web page.

Summary

● Java programs can be deployed as standalone desktop applications, which run on an appropriate version of the JRE

● Java programs can also be deployed as web page applets, which run on an appropriate version of the Java browser plugin

● Application files can be distributed for execution on other systems using the appropriate **java** interpreter

● Bundling all program files into a single JAR archive file helps ensure resource files do not become accidentally isolated

● JAR archives that are to be deployed as desktop applications must specify the program's entry point, in their manifest file

● JAR archive manifest files must have a Permissions attribute

● Executable JAR applications can be executed from a prompt with the **java -jar** command, or by clicking on their file icon

● Java programs must be digitally signed for wide distribution

● Java Web Start technology allows applications to be launched by clicking on a hyperlink on a web page

● A JNLP file stores information about a Java application in XML file format, allowing Web Start to launch that program

● Web servers must be configured to support Web Start before it can deliver Java applications across the internet

● The Java Cache Viewer can relaunch applications with Web Start, and create desktop shortcuts to run those applications

● Java applets require no window components and start from an **init** method, rather than the familiar **main** method

● Java applet parameters can be adjusted in the HTML code to allow the applet to suit its surroundings on the web page

Index